THE

Essential Skills to
Not Being a Dick | The Protocol to Lending
and Borrowing Games

CIVILIZED
GUIDE TO
TABLETOP
GAMING

RULES

EVERY GAMER

MUST LIV

Curating a
Collection

How to Be a
Good Winner and
a Better Loser

of
nes

TERI

D0950329

A **adams**media
AVON, MASSACHUSETTS

Published by
Adams Media, a division of F+W Media, Inc.
57 Littlefield Street, Avon, MA 02322. U.S.A.
www.adamsmedia.com

ISBN 10: 1-4405-9796-0
ISBN 13: 978-1-4405-9796-1
eISBN 10: 1-4405-9797-9
eISBN 13: 978-1-4405-9797-8

Printed in the United States of America.

10 9 8 7 6 5 4 3 2 1

Many of the designations used by manufacturers and sellers to
distinguish their products are claimed as trademarks. Where
those designations appear in this book and F+W Media, Inc. was
aware of a trademark claim, the designations have been printed
with initial capital letters.

Cover design by Heather McKiel.
Cover and interior images © iStockphoto.com/Aaltazar;
iStockphoto.com/Alex Belomlinsky.

This book is available at quantity discounts for bulk purchases.
For information, please call 1-800-289-0963.

CONTENTS

Introduction . . . 4

1. Your Friendly Local
Gaming Store:
The Starting Position . . . 7

2. Learning and
Teaching Games:
Be a Gaming Guru . . . 40

3. Essential Gamer
Social Skills:
Don't Be a Dick
(or Smell Like One) . . . 60

4. How to Play Games:
(So You Don't Get
Smacked Down) . . . 85

5. Gaming Groups:
Keeping Your Party
from Killing You . . . 102

6. Hosting Game Nights:
Your Martha Stewart LARP
Adventure . . . 116

7. Gaming with Family: Game
Like the Brady Bunch . . . 130

8. Tabletop Role-Playing
Game Basics: Playing Pretend
Like a Pro . . . 140

9. Attending Conventions:
Gaming with Thousands of Your
Closest Friends . . . 162

10. Talking about Games Online:
Don't Be a Troll . . . 195

11. Being a Hobby Champion:
Help Others to
Love Gaming . . . 205

Conclusion . . . 220
Acknowledgments . . . 221
Index . . . 222

INTRODUCTION

Gaming is a special gift you give yourself: It's the opportunity to create memories while doing something fun with the people who matter in your life. Unfortunately, like a disaster dinner party, it can sometimes be a way to create a special hell for yourself and others. While learning the complicated rules of some games may seem hard, harder still are mastering the unspoken rules: rules of social interaction at the gaming table, learned through painful lessons or friend-of-a-friend anecdotes told in hushed tones.

Newbie gamers may not know that cheese-dust-covered greasy snacks are a no-no food at gaming nights. That is, until they get an icy stare from their host after leaving an orange thumbprint on the special blank Cards Against Humanity card Wil Wheaton filled out and signed for him at the last comic convention.

(If you're wondering why he's mad, it's because he waited two hours in line to get that autograph, and it also cost him $40 plus the cost of parking and entry. Way to be a dick, n00b!)

While the tartrazine-coated finger situation may seem minor, there are other social gaffes that have bigger ramifications. Take, for example, the cautionary tale of Devon and Kim (not their real names).

Devon and Kim are tried-and-true gamers. They've played video games and tabletop games for many years and met and became a couple through gaming. One terrible night they and a group of friends decided to play Werewolf.

"I swear to you, I am not the werewolf." Kim said, looking Devon straight in the eye. Devon was the hunter, tasked with saving the village from the Werewolf. Kim and another friend were the last two villagers left.

"I don't believe you," replied Devon. He figuratively shot Kim with his silver bullet. Unfortunately for them and their friends, Kim was telling the truth.

It made for a very painful car ride home after the gaming session.

And if you think reading about this seems awkward, imagine being one of the other fifteen people sitting in the same room with them. Such drama does not a good gaming night make.

Games aren't just comprised of cardboard and bits of plastic, wood, or metal—they're about people. They're conduits for sharing unique experiences. Those experiences can be good, or they can be bad. The goal of this book is to show you how to make the most of each gaming experience so it's the best it can be.

After all, a tabletop game is really no good if you don't have others to play with you, even if those games come with solo-play rules.

The rules in this book will help prevent awkward and uncomfortable situations. Use these tips to try and mitigate the various minor annoyances that come from dealing with other people.

This book is a reference you can go back to again and again; you can also use it as a not-so-subtle hint to a friend to help him adjust his behavior for your next gaming night.

I've brought to bear my experience gleaned from years of being involved in tabletop gaming, having watched gaming groups fight, splinter off, or collapse; seeing great gaming hosts and poor ones; attending conventions, gaming events, and tournaments; and playing loads of late gaming nights.

This horde of tips will give you the knowledge and tools to help manage the dynamic relationships of a gaming group and gaming buddies. There are also tips and tricks for creating fun and enjoyable gaming nights, and making sure you're invited back by all those you play with. I'll help you navigate conventions, and even give you some tips to maintain and upgrade your games collection.

I wrote this book to help all gamers make the most of their gaming experiences and avoid the social unpleasantness that can also occur when you break those unspoken rules mentioned earlier. So let's get started grinding up those gaming skills—soon enough you'll have a killer proficiency bonus to all things tabletop.

1 YOUR FRIENDLY LOCAL GAMING STORE

THE STARTING POSITION

Your friendly local gaming store (FLGS) is much more than a place to buy games. It's the center of your gaming community. For that reason, it's important that you know the etiquette of behaving in it. After all:

- It's a purpose-built space where you can play games with old friends.
- It's a gathering place to meet and make new gaming friends.
- It's a venue for organized and competitive gaming events.
- It's a place that collects and curates products that can protect your games and accessories to improve your gaming experience.
- It's a place that gives you the chance to handle and try games you would otherwise never have the opportunity to play.
- It's an information resource for gaming that can recommend games specific to your tastes and likes.

Being well behaved in your FLGS isn't just a matter of politeness. It's part of the cement that holds the structure together and helps it perform all these important functions. Naturally, in supporting your FLGS you want to do it the right way. You want to be welcome each time you walk through the door and never see the staff ducking behind the counter to avoid you. In this chapter you'll learn how to become a valued member of your FLGS's community.

When I first walked into my FLGS, I saw on the shelves and walls the games that I loved and played. I saw people playing those games on the tables. I was greeted and welcomed by the staff, and nobody treated me as if I was going to steal anything. I found my favorite brand of paints to paint minis with, I talked with the people there about games I love, and I found out they were regularly gaming on days I was free. I had found my gaming home.

Part of finding a community you fit into is also knowing yourself and having the tools and vocabulary to identify the kind of gamer you are, the kinds of games you like, and the mechanics that you find engaging. Not all games are for all gamers. Knowing yourself and those you play with within your gaming community is key to all having fun, which makes the culture of your FLGS matter. You want to find players who love games you love and enjoy playing games in a way that is enjoyable to you.

Your FLGS is the heart of your local gaming community, and supporting it means supporting gaming culture where you live. The more that culture flourishes, the better it is for you as a gamer. Your FLGS will stock more games and you'll have access to more people who play. And you'll probably help a local small-business owner feed her or his family, so that smugness about fueling the engine of your nation's economy is free with each purchase.

IDENTIFY THE RIGHT FLGS FOR YOU

Finding a local gaming store seems easy—enter some basic keywords like *tabletop games store* along with where you're living into a search engine and you'll get some results. That said, finding an FLGS that is a fit for you takes a little more than that. And you have to figure out the etiquette of fitting into your FLGS. Remember: your FLGS is more than just a store; it's like an informal social club, or a bar where everyone (well, maybe not *everyone*) knows your name. You want it to be somewhere you can and would like to hang out, shop, and play games. You've gotta like the place, the people, and the culture. And they've gotta like you.

This is key: If you don't fit in with the culture of the store, you're asking for frustration, drama, and general unhappiness for both you and those around you. It's not cool. I can't emphasize enough how important it is to find a store that fits you while adapting yourself to it. If you can't find a culture that fits completely (say, because there's a limited number of choices), you can broaden the culture of a store through being a hobby champion. (You'll learn how to do this in Chapter 11.)

This only applies to those lucky people who have a choice of FLGSs. If you're traveling a league or more to get to the nearest FLGS and it is the only oasis in the proverbial gaming desert, you may not have the luxury of comparing the characteristics listed here. I hope that one day you'll be drowning in so many choices for FLGSs that you'll be glad you read over this section today.

Location

Let's start with the place. Location can mean everything.

- Can you get to it easily?
- Does it have reasonable parking, or is it accessible by public transit?
- Are the hours conducive to you being able to both shop and play there?
- Is it in a safe neighborhood where you can play in the evening without concern?

Have a look around the inside of the store. Is it clean, well lit, and spacious? Are there spaces available or dedicated to gaming within?

Talk to the staff: Are they friendly, nice, and enthusiastic about games? Do you feel respected by them? Are they knowledgeable about the store's inventory and about the gaming industry?

Every gaming store has its own focus and culture, and you should be able to tell what the focus of the store is by looking around.

- What kinds of board games does it stock, and how much of the store is dedicated to games themselves?
- Does it have a huge amount of its floor dedicated to puzzles or comics?
- Is it a miniature-gaming haven, with shelves upon shelves of tiny toy soldiers that require assembly?
- Does it offer a seemingly endless library of role-playing books, resources, and references?
- Does it sell live-action role-playing (LARP) props?

Chances are, the smaller the store is, the narrower its focus; bigger stores have the luxury of a broader selection. That doesn't mean a small store is necessarily bad; if a smaller store is offering exactly what you want, you may find it to be the right place for you. Ultimately you'll want to support a store that meets your interests. That's best for you and it's best for the store. No business owner wants a customer coming in who's perpetually dissatisfied. If you're happy with what's in the store, chances are the owners will be happy with you.

What's the Culture?

The culture of the staff and the patrons are what determines if you'll want to come back. Are they friendly? Do you feel welcomed and that you share common gaming passions? Are they helpful and enthusiastic?

You're not just shopping for a gaming store—picking your FLGS is like picking your starter gaming community, so have a good look around and support the FLGS that supports you best.

FIND THE RIGHT FLAVOR OF GAMES

There are as many kinds of games out there as there are kinds of apples. And like apples, each has a distinct flavor, texture, and use. Knowing what kinds of games there are and what they play like will help you grow and curate a collection that appeals to you. It will also help you maintain the etiquette of your gaming table, since you and your friends will know what games you all like to play and won't argue about game selection.

Again, your FLGS can help in this process. If you already know what you like to play, great! Identify a FLGS that specializes in the kinds of games you love. If you're new to gaming and not sure, find an FLGS with a wide range of games. Then start trying different games.

Different Games for Different Folks

Different kinds of games attract different kinds of people, and what you like to play probably says something important about who you are. To help you sort this out (especially if you're new to gaming), I'll briefly go through the different types of games that are out there. While this is certainly not an exhaustive list, it covers the broad categories and the best examples of each game genre.

European-Style Games
(German-Style or Eurogames)

These are board games distinguished by a few key mechanics. They usually have defined endpoints in the game with a limit to the number of player turns. Their themes tend to be economic in nature with gameplay focused on competing for scarce resources rather than military conquest. There's relatively limited interaction between the players, and not much luck is involved. The most recognizable Eurogames on the market are Ticket to Ride, the Settlers of Catan (now known as just Catan), and Carcassonne. Others include Agricola, Puerto Rico, and Caverna: The Cave Farmers.

American-Style Wargames

These often include developed themes (and possibly fully fleshed-out fictional universes), confrontational gameplay, player elimination, and moderate to high levels of luck and militaristic themes. These games offer huge opportunities for player interaction. Often, the game only ends when a single victor is declared. A hallmark of these types of games is their long play times. The most recognizable games of this type are Risk, Twilight Imperium, and Axis & Allies.

Hybrid Games or Designer Games

These games often take the best of both American-style games and Eurogames to create truly modern board games, as well as new and innovative mechanics. Examples of this still-emerging genre include Small World and Blood Rage.

Party Games

These games are designed to support gaming for larger numbers of players. Game turns are played quickly, and typical games tend to rate well for entertainment, engagement, and accessibility (the rules tend to be simpler) but lower in terms of strategy.

Werewolf, the Resistance, and Cards Against Humanity are the most widely played party games and are readily available at most FLGSs.

Collectible Games

Collectible games are those played using personal collections that are compiled into a constructed format. Collectible card games are often card games (the format began with a collectible card game back in 1993), though they may also include other collectibles such as miniatures or dice. Magic: The Gathering, Pokémon Trading Card Game, and Yu-Gi-Oh! Trading Card Game are the most common collectible card games on the market, while HeroClix and Dice Masters dominate the non-card-game aspect of this genre.

Tabletop Role-Playing Games (RPGs)

These are a unique type of tabletop game. The components are less important than the players' imaginations and problem-solving skills. The game is facilitated for the players by a game master (GM) or dungeon master (DM)—titles that are used interchangeably. This person articulates the universe, situations, and outcomes for the players based on their reactions and dice rolls. The most popular tabletop RPGs are Dungeons & Dragons (D&D) and Pathfinder.

Miniature Tabletop Gaming

In the past this genre was concerned with recreating historical battles. Now it's evolved to also include science-fiction and fantasy universes. The play and collecting style is similar to that

THE OLDEST HOBBY GAMES

Miniatures are some of the oldest games in the hobby game industry. In 1913, the science-fiction writer H.G. Wells published *Little Wars*, a book of rules for playing with military miniatures. In fact, the full title was *Little Wars (A Game for Boys from twelve years of age to one hundred and fifty and for that more intelligent sort of girl who likes boys' games and books).*

of collectible card games, though game expansions are not blind boosters; rather, gamers can see what minis they're buying.

The most popular miniature games are Games Workshop's Warhammer games (Warhammer 40,000, Warhammer Age of Sigmar), Star Wars: X-Wing Miniatures Game, and Privateer Press's Warmachine and Hordes. Hybrid board game/miniatures games include Zombicide, Blood Rage, and Star Wars: Imperial Assault.

With a plethora of games out there, there's something for everyone. Now that you know the types of games you're likely to find in your FLGS, it only remains for you to figure out what kind you and your friends like to play.

Most FLGSs will run demos of various games, have community gaming days where players can bring and run games from their collections, or stock a library of games that players can try themselves before they buy. *Take advantage of these opportunities as much as you can.* Hobby dollars are scarce, so take the time before you spend them, and curate your personal collection so it's only full of things you truly love.

UNDERSTAND THE GAME MECHANICS WHEN YOU'RE PLAYING

Every game is built around a set of core mechanics. Knowing the mechanics of a game will give you a better sense of how much you and, often more importantly, your gaming group will enjoy the game. As well—and this is important—you won't annoy your fellow players by endlessly asking someone to explain why you're rolling a ten-sided die instead of a twenty-sided die or how many land cards you have to tap before summoning a goblin.

One of the first things to do is decide what kinds of games all of you like to play. If your gaming group is a bunch of strategic players accustomed to action drafting, they may not have the same appreciation for a subjective player-judged game, and vice versa. Picking the right games for you and your group is good manners, and it's the key to having good, enjoyable gaming nights.

To that end, here's a short list of common mechanics, as well as the vocabulary of popular games. You can use this to impress the staff at your FLGS, and it'll help you best choose games that fit you and your group.

Deck Building/Pool Construction

Most exemplified by games like Dice Masters and Magic: The Gathering, as well as the majority of miniature war games, these terms refer to players collecting a pool and building a list unique to them from that collection. The fun is in both trying to build an optimized list from what's available to you and seeing if the list performs as you anticipate it will.

Luck

The amount of luck varies from game to game. Knowing your tolerance as well as that of your group's for the amount of luck in a game is very useful when deciding what you're going to play. For the sake of ease, luck is defined as anything that isn't directly in the control of at least one player. Here's an easy scale: Chess has no luck, Scrabble has moderate amounts of luck, Yahtzee has substantial amounts of luck, and Snakes and Ladders is pure luck.

Bluffing

Deception is an extremely old gaming mechanic (think poker or other card games) whose use in modern games allows players themselves to become an element of the mechanics of the game. Players and groups that appreciate bluffing mechanics are those who enjoy outwitting each other as much as they like playing the game itself. Diplomacy, for example, is a game in which bluffing (and bargaining) plays a big role.

Cooperation

Games with cooperative elements are terrific options for team building and bonding. Games that are fully cooperative (meaning that everyone wins or loses together) tend to be very challenging. A subset of cooperative games are partly cooperative games, meaning there may be individual players with separate victory conditions that may be achieved either in tandem with the group's goal or work contrary to it. Dungeons & Dragons is a fully cooperative game in which the players are working together to survive perils and accumulate treasure and experience points. Pandemic is a cooperative board game in which the players work together to stop the spread of diseases.

THE CONFUSED GAMER

Here's an example of why it's polite to understand game mechanics before you sit down at the gaming table:

A group of friends have just started playing the classic Dungeons & Dragons module White Plume Mountain. As Charlotte, the dungeon master, sets up the first encounter, Kevin, a player new to the group, sits poking nervously through his dice.

Charlotte: Okay. As you round the corner, you see a group of goblins ahead. What do you do?

Players: We rush toward them, weapons drawn.

Charlotte: Okay. Everyone roll for initiative.

Kevin: What's that mean?

Charlotte: It means we have to decide who takes an action first.

Kevin: Oh. How do we do that?

Charlotte: Roll a d10.

Kevin: What's that?

Charlotte: Uh . . . a ten-sided die.

Kevin: I don't think I have one of those.

Rich (exasperated): Oh, for God's sake! It's right there! Don't play the game if you don't know anything about how to play it!

Not a very good start to a fun evening of gaming, is it? Kevin ended up sulking the rest of the evening, and his group could probably brush up on the rules for teaching games (conveniently found within this book).

Action Drafting and Worker Placement

Worker placement games, also referred to as action drafting games, offer players a set of options for action but limit the number of choices a single player can make and how many times a single choice may be made in a round. These games tend to be strategic and sit on the lower end of the luck spectrum. Agricola, Settlers of Catan (and its variants), and Lords of Waterdeep exemplify this mechanic.

Storytelling

Games that have a storytelling mechanic provide game immersion more than strategy. Some storytelling games, such as RPGs, don't provide a single clear winner. But they can be immersive and accessible to novice and nongamers as they are beloved by experienced gamers. In addition to D&D and Pathfinder, popular story-based games include the Firefly RPG from Margaret Weis Productions and Numenera from Monte Cook Games.

Elimination

There are a lot of older games whose elimination mechanics made the game boring and terrible (Monopoly and Risk come to mind). Contemporary use of the elimination is generally combined with light and fast gameplay—meaning players who are eliminated can watch entertaining gameplay, at which point the game is wrapped and can be replayed again. These contemporary elimination games also often feature unique themes and fantastic art. Games such as Exploding Kittens and Get Bit! are paragons of elimination-centered games.

Player Judging

Sometimes the best part of playing a game is the sound of players' laughter, and some games are designed purely around that outcome. (Some gamers, on the other hand, are deadly serious and rarely crack a smile; decide which kind of gamer you are before sitting down to a gaming session.) Games that have a player-judging element for best responses, best answers, or simply best failures are designed to reward players for delighting their friends, sometimes through self-deprecation, like in Cards Against Humanity; sometimes through wit, like in Funemployed; and sometimes through both. These games aren't satisfying to strategic and competitive gamers, but they often encompass the best of what games offer: fun for all. When laughs are had, everyone wins.

At the end of the day, if you know the kinds of things you and your gaming pals appreciate (and revile), you'll be better able to choose the kinds of games that make fun gaming nights rather than ones that fail to please. That's what real victory feels like—everyone having fun.

BALANCE THE NEEDS OF YOU AND YOUR FRIENDS

Knowing yourself and those you play with are the last parts of the equation when picking games. The things that make games fun for some people may not be appealing (and may actually be off-putting) to other gamers. It's basic gamer etiquette to be self-aware and know something about your fellow players. After all, that's one of the things that makes gaming fun—you're interacting with other people, and by doing so you're gaining self-knowledge.

If you know what kinds of things engage you and your gaming group, you'll all be able to come together and play games in the same spirit and with the same mentality. I'll say it plainly: Sometimes as gamers we turn into monsters. If everyone around the table turns into the same kind of monster when playing a game, the game is fun—everyone is playing with the same intent, expectation, and intensity.

It's when there's a discrepancy in that intent, expectation, and intensity around the table that things go sour. That makes for a bad gaming night with sullen gamers, the possibility of hurt feelings, and social friction that can extend beyond the end of the game.

The key is to find games that will engage everyone relatively well. Games that have broad appeal work well, but even if one or two gamers are particularly engaged by a single game and the rest are moderately engaged, that's fine. The thing you don't want is a game that completely puts off one or more of the people around the table; if that happens, you may ultimately lose them.

These elements of engagement will help pick a game (or several games) that can be played and will appeal to everyone at the table, so everyone has an enjoyable time. Find out how much your fellow players enjoy (or hate) these elements.

Crunchiness and Weightiness

Some games are really complex to master and are just plain hard to win. The term "crunchiness" is used to describe how challenging a game is to learn, win, and master and how much strategy is required to play. Some people refer to a game in terms of "weight" to describe how involved gamers need to be to play. A heavy game is one that is deeply involving, requiring heavy strategy and considered hard. A light game is one that is much less so.

Games high in crunch are appealing to those willing to put in the time to develop the mastery. They can be less so for players who are new, particularly when up against those who have had a chance to climb the (typically steep) learning curve. Some novice players may enjoy the challenge, but those who don't like losing won't have a good time.

Games that are lighter (sometimes referred to as "fluffy") are easily played, quickly learned, and often don't take as much time. Gamers who prefer heavy gaming experiences may not feel satisfied playing lighter games.

Action and Adventure

Adventure games unfold a story for all the players to experience. Such games not only provide players a narrative to follow but also give them a sense of achievement, rewarding players with unique items, abilities, and other game-specific perks.

Adventure games can be rich and immersive, but on the flip side sometimes they require a heavy time investment. You can't really have a great adventure game in a fifteen-minute window. Casual gamers may lose interest or fall off.

Stress

Some games are intentionally built to put pressure on players. These are games that elicit stress in the gamers, making them feel urgency and tension. Zombicide is a case where the stress of the game escalates as you watch your paths to your objectives and exit point fill with zombies too numerous to kill, shambling toward you in a slow, creeping wall of death. This kind of intensive action can be immersive to players who like that kind of edge-of-your-seat play, but players who don't like feeling constantly stressed and exhausted at the end of a game may not enjoy such games.

On the other hand, to gamers who enjoy a rush of adrenaline, games that do not have a stress element can sometimes feel somewhat pedantic in play. Players who enjoy the fury of stress-inducing games can get bored if a game doesn't have the right amount of tension.

Creativity

Every game needs some degree of creativity, but the kind of creativity required varies greatly from game to game. From problem-solving to strategy execution to wit and humor, how games engage the creative part of the players' brains is important. A strategy-loving player may find a game based purely on wit and humor vapid, whereas a group that loves puns might thoroughly enjoy a player-judged pun battle game.

Think about tailoring your game choices to your group's preferences using these categories to vet the kinds of games that will have the most appeal across all the gamers in your group so everyone can have a great time.

CURATE YOUR COLLECTION — THINK BEFORE YOU BUY

There's one simple rule to follow before you buy a game: Try it before you buy it. Great art, a well-known game designer, enticing descriptions on the back of the box, and fancy components may entice you to buy a game, but if it sits on your shelf, it does you more harm than good, since it's taking up valuable shelf real estate and eating into your limited hobby budget.

There's a rule in my house: A game must reach the Galaxy Trucker metric of fun to be purchased. This completely arbitrary metric uses a single game, Galaxy Trucker, as the measure for whether or not a game meets our tastes for fun, play time, and replayability.

Here are things you will want to consider before you spend your cash on that new game you've got your eyes on.

The Fun Factor

Consider whether or not the game is fun to you and whether it would be fun for people you regularly game with. It may be a great game for you, but if it won't appeal to the people you hope to play with, the chances are pretty high that it will sit on your shelf.

Having a good idea about what kinds of games you like and what mechanics most appeal to you will help you more easily weigh a game's fun factor.

The Setup and Takedown Factor

When trying a game to figure out if you want to buy it, look at the time spent in setting it up and taking it down. Examine the number of components required and how easy or involved the setup is. Generally speaking, the more involved the game's setup is, the more complex and involved the gameplay. That isn't always the case, but games that have a very involved setup but very short gameplay are generally ones you won't play—the upfront investment is too high, particularly if a game takes half as long to set up as it does to play.

Also consider that a game that takes a decent amount of time to set up will also take a decent chunk of time to put away (sometimes if you're doing it right, it takes more time to put away than set up). So evaluate that aspect of the game as well.

My rule for most board games is that I'm cool with one minute of setup for ten minutes of gameplay, to a maximum of fifteen minutes of setup. If a game takes more than fifteen minutes from the time the box is opened to the start of gameplay, in my opinion it takes too long. That rule varies with other types of games, particularly miniature war games, but knowing my general tolerances has helped me curate my own collection. Your own tolerance obviously will vary.

Game Length

The amount of time a game takes to play will affect how often you will play it. That doesn't mean that long-playing games don't have a place in a collection or aren't enjoyable, but before you spend cold hard cash on a game that takes four hours to play, take a moment to consider not only whether the game is enjoyable enough to spend four hours playing it but also how many friends you'll be able to regularly convince to play it with you.

My own collection includes small-box games (some of which play in fifteen to twenty minutes) that I tend to play with my casual gaming friends and family all the way to meaty war games that take two to three hours to play. Those are played with my circle of mini war gamers, who are accustomed to that kind of gaming experience and structure their lives around regular gaming nights. If you don't have friends with that kind of dedication, consider games that will fit into both your life and theirs.

The Cost Factor

Some games are more expensive than others. Import costs for certain games, high-quality components, fiddly bits that are costly to produce—all of these may increase the cost of a game. You've got to be able to justify the cost and measure whether the purchase is worth it for you.

One of the ways I think about a game is whether I'll get an hour of enjoyment from the game for every dollar I'll be spending on it. I spend the time to paint the minis in many of my games, so games with miniatures are worth the higher cost, but that may not be the case for you, and the extra toys inside a box may not be as worthwhile.

Ultimately you want a collection of well-used and well-loved games rather than a pile of shame hidden in the back of a closet.

STORE SMART: MANAGING AND STORING GAMES AND THEIR EXPANSIONS

Most games often come in their own storage container. Storing them on a shelf in their box simply makes sense. However, some games, particularly those with expansions, complicate this simple storage system. For games that have expansions that come neatly in their own boxes, it can be a hassle to re-box them, especially if those additions become permanent staples of your game play (like the various expansions of Machi Koro and Small World). Furthermore, many expansions come in blister packs or expansions you'd rather store with the core game (like those for table-top minis games like X-Wing Miniatures Game, Ninja All Stars, or Zombicide). Other games are expanded in blind boosters (like all collectible games). For games with contents that can't be well stored for whatever reason, there are a variety of solutions beyond trying to salvage old shoeboxes to put your components in. And nothing undermines the coolness of a full shelf of games quicker than a beat-up shoebox.

Option 1: Clear Bead Boxes/Plano Boxes

For games that have a good deal of miniatures, tokens, and other components that can't practically be stored and transported easily in their original packaging (like Star Wars: X-Wing Miniatures Game), go to your local hardware store or craft store and purchase clear bead or plano boxes. These clear boxes are a great way to store and organize your collection and offer the additional benefit that you'll be able to see exactly what's inside each case.

Option 2: Box Inserts and Organizers

Companies like the Broken Token and Go7 Gaming make great box inserts that are custom cut for a variety of games so you not only can keep all the components organized and separated within the box without the use of ziptop bags, but also allow you to fit the expansions of the games inside the core box set. If you don't want to buy a box insert, you can usually craft one yourself with a little help from online tutorials.

Option 3: Blank Wooden Boxes

I have a particular soft spot for blank sliding-lid boxes I acquire from Etsy, particularly for smaller box games with boxes that tend to get beat up from transport and that tend to be a little too big for the contents. You can put multiple games in one of these boxes, then either label them, customize them (using the old boxes and some Mod Podge to decoupage labels), or even paint them to identify their contents. They look stylish while also offering excellent protection for your small-box games.

Game storage is both a practical skill as well as an aesthetic one—the way you sort and display your games makes it easier for you to grab the one you want. It's extremely convenient to have all of a game's components at your fingertips while also making it easier to transport and store the games you love enough to bring to your FLGS, a nearby café, or your friends' homes to play.

PAY WHERE YOU PLAY

An FLGS is so much more than a store—it's a community hub, a place you can network with other gamers, a place where you can get curated recommendations, and somewhere you can actually play games. It goes without saying that there are a few things that are just poor form to do. Here are a handful of unspoken rules that you should keep in mind when dealing with your FLGS.

Support Your FLGS

Your FLGS is owned by real people and staffed by people who legitimately love games. But that also means that those real people need sales in their store to do things like keep the lights on or feed themselves and their families. So if you play in a store, or use the expertise of the staff for recommendations, don't buy your games elsewhere. Pay where you play.

Don't Expect to Get Online Prices at a Brick-and-Mortar Store

A brick-and-mortar store has costs that online retailers don't have. Take, for example, the square footage most stores dedicate to gaming that is generally provided for free to the gaming community. Most local retailers have to lease their retail space by the square foot, so space dedicated to gaming has an actual cost associated with it. That doesn't even take into account heating and cooling costs to keep patrons comfortable or things like washroom supplies (again, for the comfort of the gamers in the store).

Consider this: If you like the staff who work at the store, you hope they're earning a decent living wage. That's pretty much impossible if brick-and-mortar stores match online prices. Some stores even do things like run free demo days or offer painting lessons for game miniatures, again with various costs associated.

Hopefully all those little niceties that your FLGS offers makes the slightly higher prices more than worthwhile. You can't really put a price on having a great atmosphere to play games or a resource for solid game advice.

Don't Smell

I'll admit this might not be an *unspoken* rule at your FLGS. I'll cover why this might be and how to handle it fully in Chapter 3: Essential Gamer Social Skills, but simply put, mind your hygiene. Like culture, it's also in your hands (or pits).

Be Respectful

Talk to the store owner or staff if you have suggestions or concerns. Here's the coolest thing about your FLGS: The staff and the store owners are literally invested in making the store a great place for people to be. If you have suggestions or concerns, you can always just talk to them. This is no weird "tell us how we did" suggestion box, where feedback goes into the ether. Rather, there's a real human who will take your suggestions into consideration.

Don't expect the store to change just to accommodate your wishes, but if you have ideas to make your FLGS a better place, go ahead and communicate them. I've done things ranging from recommending hobby products I felt my FLGS should carry to talking to the owners about running more organized events. They're responsive, and even if they don't do exactly what I'd want, they take my concerns seriously and try to accommodate my suggestions. This is why I say that you set the culture in your FLGS—because you as much as anyone else have a hand in creating it.

When it comes to getting on well within a gaming store, the big points to keep in mind are to be respectful of the space and the staff, considerate of the other patrons, and thoughtful of the kind of community you want to support and foster. That's ultimately what these rules are about.

HOST GAMES AT YOUR FLGS
THE RIGHT WAY

If you want to get into gaming and hosting games but your home isn't well suited to gaming, there is a fantastic way to jump in. Many gaming stores have a purpose-built space for gaming. Why not take advantage of this? It's also a great way to get more visibility for a game you like but that isn't commonly played, since people in the gaming store will be wandering by and seeing how the game works.

There is, however, a right way and a wrong way to do it. You want to be sure to follow proper protocol so you and everyone else have a good time.

Ask Your FLGS If You Can Host a Game
and When the Best Day Would Be

You're using their space, so you'll need to ask permission to host a game. Most FLGSs are pretty cool about people running games in their space. Knowing the best time, however, can be a bit of a tricky dance. A lot of stores run regular events on most days of the week, and these take up most if not all their space on those nights. Asking which days are best means you won't get stomped on by gamers who expect to use their space on their days.

Make Sure It's a Game
That Your FLGS Stocks

It's a bit of a douchebag move to play a game in a gaming store that doesn't sell that particular game. That said, sometimes stores are just happy to encourage people to play, so it never hurts to ask, especially if it's a game the store can bring in but hasn't because the staff wasn't familiar with it and nobody expressed an interest. If you get a no, don't be salty about it. It's mega weird to play a game you can't say you bought at the store (see the rule about paying where you play).

The other thing you want to check is if the store is okay with the game you want to play at their tables. As popular as Cards Against Humanity is, it's not a game that is especially family friendly. If the store is oriented to families, including small children, that might not be a great game to play there.

Broadcast That You're Gaming at Your FLGS

Checking in on your social media networks, letting people know you're playing at your FLGS, and broadcasting that you will be gaming there is a way to let people know about your FLGS, your favorite games, and how cool your FLGS is with you playing your fave games in their store. Helping to share the love of the hobby, not only by elevating awareness about gaming but also the venues for gaming, is what all the cool kids do. So be a cool kid.

There are downsides to gaming in your FLGS; having to adhere to store hours and working around previously scheduled events are the biggest ones. But having a central place for you and your friends to play, where you don't have to worry about the number of chairs or if your table is big enough, or what happens if Kevin forgot his dice again (he can just go and buy some more), is pretty fantastic. And it's a service that helps the staff get more people in the store and playing games. Take advantage of it.

SIDE NOTE ON GETTING THE BEST BANG FOR YOUR BUCK AT YOUR FLGS

This isn't really a rule—just a little secret: Because an FLGS can't match online prices doesn't mean you can't get a great deal from it. Here are a few ways you can stretch those hobby dollars while still supporting the place you play.

1. *See if your FLGS offers bundle prebuys or bundle deals.* Some FLGSs have great prebuy deals for new releases of games or bundle deals. My FLGS gives discounts if people buy collectible boosters in larger quantities. Inquire about it.

2. *Sign up for your FLGS's loyalty program if it has one.* Some stores offer a points system allowing customers to bank up points based on purchases that they can then use for discounts, free products, or other cool rewards for shopping at the store. Brick-and-mortar gaming stores know that they're competing with online stores, so many of them reward customers who shop with them. Ask your FLGS if it has one.

3. *See if publishers are rewarding customers for shopping at an FLGS.* If your favorite publisher has a newsletter, sign up for it, because sometimes they'll reward customers who shop for their products at FLGSs. Companies like Privateer Press and Wyrd will occasionally send free stuff to customers who send photos of their receipts when they buy the publisher's

products. I've gotten free limited-run items from publishers for shopping at my FLGS. That's pretty darned cool.

4. *Play in organized events at your store.* Participating in events at your FLGS is a great way to get a little extra for the cost of product you were going to buy anyway. In booster-draft organized events, often there's a small discount offered for the bundle of boosters you need to buy to get into the game. For other games, there are sometimes prizes for players who participate, including participation prizes, which are otherwise unavailable outside of organized play. It's a great opportunity to play games as well as get a little something extra.

5. *Sales are still a thing.* If your FLGS has an e-mail newsletter or a Facebook page, subscribe to that. Newsletters often let you know about deals going on in the store, and being looped into those can help you make your hobby dollars go a little longer.

6. *Split a purchase with a friend.* There are a lot of starter games that can be split—particularly those that are deck/pool building or are otherwise collectible. Buying in with a friend and splitting the contents is an economical way to make your dollars go further, and something you could not do if you were buying online: There is no board game eHarmony out there to help you find an online match to split a box, without also eventually costing you money in shipping. Even local online groups are a product of strong gaming stores that have invested in the gaming culture, and your local FLGS is a pretty easy place to meet up to split a box (and maybe even start playing it right away).

Just because you're helping to do things like keep the lights on in a gaming space by paying higher prices than found on Amazon doesn't mean there aren't ways to get more toys for less money. Plus the staff and the patrons at your FLGS will do things like laugh at your bad jokes because they like you, which is something that Amazon can never do.

CHECK YOUR ATTITUDE AT THE DOOR

The community and culture of a gaming store is defined by both the staff and the patrons, which means you. If every member of the community has a creative, respectful attitude toward the FLGS and its patrons, that's great. Sadly, too often it's uncommon.

I'll be blunt: Being a dick in the store means poisoning that culture, and there's no room for that. Instead, be a force of positivity when it comes to encouraging gaming and other gamers. Be willing to learn, and be willing to teach when you play games in the store or get into conversations with other people. By being the best that gaming has to offer in the store, you're investing in a gaming culture that you'll benefit from in the future. You are ensuring that other people will also support the store, and you're making certain you'll have a place to game for a long time to come.

First and foremost, you are not entitled to any more or less special treatment than any other gamer. Every rule applies to every person equally, whether that's within a game or within the game store. Just because you spend x number of dollars in a store doesn't mean you're entitled to act as though you're better than anyone else who walks through the door of your FLGS, even if that person has never spent a dollar. The special person is the one who treats all gamers and patrons as though they're special.

You're Not Always Right

Don't be the jerk who is always right. I've seen gamers who have been playing a particular game for years find out that they've been playing a game wrong—sometimes from someone who doesn't have the same stake in the game. Your own investment (time or money) in a game doesn't make you always right. Everyone else's opinions and perspectives are equally valid.

When it comes to conflicting interpretations of the rules, there are always ways to keep the game moving forward (even if it's a dice roll). Not every rulebook covers every scenario, and when rules conflict it's better to be gaming than it is to be right. When it comes to conflicting opinions, a differing one from your own doesn't negate your perspective. There's room in this world for people who believe Twilight Imperium is the best game ever, as well as people who would rather lose toenails painfully than be forced to play it.

Finally, don't treat your FLGS as though it's a private club for you and your friends. Insofar as you've got such a place, it's your dining room table, or your basement. It's not a public store. That means being welcoming to new people who express an interest in playing games with you. It also means helping them find their own path within a game rather than imposing your own views on them.

One gentleman I eventually became close friends with would consistently denigrate my purchasing decisions for a particular army in a game he had been playing for years. I was just starting it, and his comments not only insulted my decisions but also insulted my intelligence for liking them. It wasn't cool, but eventually we worked things out. You don't want to be the person who has to be publicly called out in order for your dickish behavior to be forgiven.

2 LEARNING AND TEACHING GAMES

BE A GAMING GURU

Gamers need to learn how to play games, and sometimes that's not the easiest thing to do. The fact of the matter is that learning games and teaching games can be really, really hard. Rules can be complicated, poorly written, or just plain confusing. They're a set of instructions that are often provided without context. When you learn and teach a game, what you're really doing is understanding and articulating the context and the mechanics simultaneously.

It sounds so simple, but in fact it's an extremely challenging thing to do.

As a player, you may be faced with having to do things like chew through twenty pages of rules, understand them, digest them, and regurgitate them in a way that is meaningful to a group of friends.

You may end up being completely confused before you get to popping out the cardboard components in the box. If you get through that, you may have to do a better job than the game's instructions, teaching the game to others without overwhelming and discouraging them.

In my experience, teaching a new game to people who have never heard or seen it before is about as easy as trying to walk a tightrope while juggling flaming torches. If you don't have the tools to make a game seem easy and fun, the chances are you won't be playing it with your friends tonight. And that would suck royally.

I vividly recall a failed attempt to both simultaneously learn and teach a complicated game to a less-than-attentive audience. It was a late-night gaming session; a friend had just acquired a game he was excited to play but wasn't particularly familiar with. It was still wrapped in cellophane. As we sat around a table popping out the *hundreds* of tiny cardboard tokens, setting up the *dozens* of components, and trying to make sense of the gaming aids with tired, bleary eyes, he was trying to decipher the rules compiled in a forty-page book. To the surprise of nobody, the game did not happen. (To be honest, there was a bit of a drunken mutiny against the game after one frustrated and inebriated friend decided that a game that took fifteen minutes to pop out all the components and get them set up was not the right game for that time of night or that level of intoxication. He was right.)

This chapter will show you how to learn games quickly so you can spool up and politely and successfully teach your friends how to play them. The next time you buy a new game, the thought of teaching it and playing it with friends for the first time should fill you with excitement, not dread.

TRANSLATE RULES TO GAMES

Here's the unfortunate truth: Many of the classic Eurogame instructions weren't written in English. Many of them come from Germany, and when they were exported to this country, some of the rules weren't perfectly translated. Furthermore, sometimes these games didn't have great instructions to begin with. As well, in some games that are a little more aged, the rules sometimes aren't very clear.

Often, game instructions are self-referential as though the game exists in a vacuum, but game designers themselves do not design games in a vacuum. I've known games to assume the players would know the game's most basic mechanics, but never actually outlined those mechanics. In some sets of game instructions, there's a cultural gap between the game's designers and its American audience.

All of this means that you have to be able to serve as an intermediary between the rules as they're written and your friends to whom you're trying to explain them. Here are four rules to navigating those leaps in translation and culture:

1. Visit the publisher's website. Sometimes there are support documents (like rules clarifications and FAQs for games). Look for those to get context.
2. Look for how-to-play instructional videos and gameplay videos online. When trying to get context, sometimes a video is far better at articulating a particular game mechanic than a rulebook is. I have a particular fondness

for Watch It Played on YouTube—there's something to be said about seeing how a game is played that crystallizes and clarifies understanding better than rereading a set of instructions.

3. Play the game wrong. Sometimes you just need to start rolling dice and try to play the game, however incorrectly, then reread the rules after to get an understanding of what you did wrong. You need the context of the game to actually understand what's going on. If you're a more experienced gamer, sometimes you'll feel like something is being played wrong because it doesn't feel intuitive. That's a good hint to reread the rules about that particular mechanic. That intuition has helped me identify things I'm playing incorrectly or my own gaps in understanding the rules. Even if that gap isn't covered, feeling you're doing something wrong means you can articulate it when you go to other support sources (like BoardGameGeek's forums or the publisher's website).

4. Sometimes the rules just fail and you can't figure out the right answer. In those cases, play the game in a way that feels the most fair and enjoyable: optimize for happiness. It's more important to kludge a rule that feels right and apply it consistently.

Learning games isn't so much a task as it is a process, and when you're dealing with a translated game, sometimes that process has a few more steps. That's fine—just keep reaching out and looking for the answers, and if all else fails, play it in a way that makes you happy.

MAKE YOUR OWN GAMING AIDS

Let's be straight: Some games have complicated, finicky, or otherwise involved mechanics that are challenging to remember.

That doesn't make them bad or unpleasant—some of my favorite games have really in-depth rules that even I still can't remember off the top of my own head.

Games like that are fun, but sometimes having your own crib sheet or other gaming aids to help you remember what's going on or what's to be done next can substantially improve the flow of a game, letting you and your friends better enjoy it. That's particularly true if there are newbies present who haven't played the game or don't have your experience with gaming. Game aids can help these people feel comfortable and confident.

There's no shame in having personal references for your game. So here are a few things I tend to find especially useful when I've got a complicated game and I want all of us at the table to know what we're doing.

Turn-Sequence Reference

Outlining the various steps in a turn sequence helps keep things straight when you're playing, so you don't have to try to reverse-engineer a turn of a game because you did something wrong earlier in the turn.

Having this reference keeps you from skipping an important step as well, whether that's a game turn sequence or for an individual player's turn.

Keep it simple—write down the general actions or make a photocopy of the part of the rules that summarizes each turn and give a copy to all the players so everyone is always on the same page and can reference these rules without having to continually ask for the rulebook.

Tokens and Counters

Easy-to-make counters and tokens help for tracking health points, resources, or scoring.

There's something about having a visual cue to mark things, like how much damage or wounds have been taken in a game, what effects might be on a particular character, or what the score is in a game.

Some games include meeples or other tracking items, but many don't. If you're finding you need to track certain things (like health points, scoring points, or special effects), there are a number of easy aids you can use.

Some of the easiest-to-access tokens for counting up or down are decorative beads and stones available at local dollar stores. They're useful for marking what things have been moved or activated, how many points of damage something has taken, or even marking who went first in a particular turn.

MAKE YOUR OWN VERSUS ALREADY MADE

A lot of game manufacturers include reference cards in the game, especially if it's complicated. I certainly wouldn't discourage you from using them, but your own aids can speak specifically to things you have issues remembering. There's no reason you can't use both.

I also like using dice to count up or down, particularly if the values get high. Any hobby store worth its salt will carry standard four-sided (d4), six-sided (d6), eight-sided (d8), ten-sided (d10), and twenty-sided (d20) dice at the very least, though if you ask around you might find yourself some fun polyhedral dice like the unusual d7s and d11s.

Last but not least, bottle caps and lids and pennies, paired with either a permanent marker or a dry-erase pen, make for great markers for noting various effects. If something is slow, blinded, poisoned, or knocked down and the game didn't include tokens (which is common for many miniature games as well as role-playing games), it helps to have a bag full of bottle caps you can write the effect on and use as a reminder of the effect.

Reference Cards

A stack full of index cards is super helpful in a variety of games. If there's a particular effect or damage table you need to refer to in a game, having it on an index card is very useful.

If you have a bunch of magic spells or items that have unique abilities but you need to continually reference the rulebook for them, having those effects and abilities on an index card to reference is helpful.

I always keep a stack of index cards and pencils nearby whenever gaming night shows up. When I find that I'm continually referencing something in the rulebook, or I think a particular section is useful, I'll make myself a reference card for future use. Chances are if you need it to reference, someone else will too.

Be polite and share your cards with the group. Others may make reference cards that you find helpful. Sharing helps all of you enjoy the game more and be more attuned to its nuances.

Making gaming aids for yourself and your group is useful, particularly if you find yourself constantly referencing the main rules. Focus on things you're finding hard to remember but are important, things that are unintuitive, or things that just help the game flow. The small effort you put in when making these aids will give you a return in time saved when you play the game.

PICK THE RIGHT GAME
FOR YOUR GROUP

In the previous chapter I mentioned that if you're going to start teaching games to your group, you're going to need to know what kinds of games they'll want to play to begin with.

The first step to picking the right game is making sure that whatever game you pick, you can sell the idea to your group. Sometimes premise and theme can carry you a long way. It's easier to articulate a context for the game if there's a clear theme that helps you encapsulate the game.

You can get a very clear idea by summing up a game's theme to yourself. Without knowing the mechanics, you should be able to know if you and your group would be more excited to play a game where you pretend to be midcentury European diplomats negotiating and battling to define the borders of a continent (Diplomacy), or if you'd rather play as a group of intergalactic cargo haulers who have to deal with space pirates and asteroids (Galaxy Trucker).

Neither of those descriptions describe these games from a mechanics standpoint, but the theme can capture imagination and interest in a way that mechanics may not. That doesn't mean mechanics doesn't have a hand in keeping interest, though. It's the next thing you should weigh. Would the group rather play a game in which you manage resources for maximum productivity (Agricola), or one in which you compete head to head for territory on the earth and moon (Risk 2210 A.D.)? Or would the group prefer a game in which the players battle the game itself for victory (Pandemic)?

The nature of the gamers you're dealing with will determine the kinds of games you'll be playing. If you're playing with a group of people who love the history of war but dislike confrontation in their games, a cooperative war game like The Grizzled would serve you well, as opposed to a historical tabletop war game.

So look at your gamers and figure out if they're more likely to be Care Bears or vanquishers, storytellers or puzzle masters, comedians or trolls. If you can determine that, you'll likely have more success picking the right game for your group.

TEACH YOUR GAME WELL

You've read the rules, you've picked the game, now it's time to teach it.

Take a breath. Start with explaining how players win. Brevity matters here. Focus on the one metric that determines victory. "We win if we complete the objective and all get out without having zombies eat our faces." Or, "The winner is the person who scores the most at the end of the game."

Break down a single game turn so all the players know how the turn sequence should go. While explaining the turn sequence, introduce *some* of the various actions a player can do and briefly resolve them.

One more thing: Try to make your explanations fun and humorous. The point is to make the experience of gameplay fun. Even when you're being talked at for five minutes straight, that part can still be fun if you, the teacher, inject a little bit of humor. Also, people tend to remember things better when they think they're funny. You may not need to make jokes, but throw in some pop culture references, some terrible puns, or some sound effects and you'll be surprised how well the players will respond. If you feel foolish, remember you're playing with grown-up toys and it's best not to take yourself seriously.

Play an Open Hand

It may also help to play an open hand showing all the components you're referencing. Make the moves the players might make. Furthermore, be sure to go through the beginning and end phases of each turn, not just the player phases.

Let me be clear: When explaining the process of taking a turn, it shouldn't take more than five minutes. Be very brief, gloss over the tiny details, and just explain the game in broad strokes. This

---

PLAYING THE GAME

Here's an example of what you might say: "The first player will take two actions. Let's say they walk and then open this door. This is how we figure out how far she can walk—we look here on her card. After that, if we look at what kind of weapon she's holding, we can see if she can use it to open doors. Turns out, axes are good at opening doors. Now, the second player can then take his two actions. Let's say he walks into the room the first player opened the door to, and then he tries to blow that zombie's head off with his gun. Sure, he has a frying pan in the other hand, but I endorse the shooting choice because frying pans don't kill zombies; people with guns do.

"The gun has a 2 on its rate of fire stat, and 4+ as its hit stat, which you can see on the weapon card. So he'll roll two dice and kill that zombie if one of them shows a 4 or higher. The third player can walk into the room and search for some food because that's on the objective list. She'll just draw from the item deck to search. If we're lucky, it's not cat food, but we're not picky; it's the apocalypse.

"After everyone has gone, we then see if more zombies spawn, which is inevitable because we have brains and they're brainetarians. We'll determine how many come up and where they'll show up, and then that's the turn."

---

is because at this point you're still selling the idea of playing this game. If you lose players while explaining the game to them, they'll never buy in.

After that, it's time to play a coached version of the game. The big thing is to let players take their turns but give them insight at the start of their turn as to what actions they can take. Explain to them some basic strategies as they move through their turn.

The players haven't yet played the game, but now they have a clearer picture of what's happening, and you're not throwing rules at them completely out of context.

One other hint: Look at the players while you explain stuff. Their faces will tell you if they're getting what you're saying or if you need to walk them through particular mechanics again. Gently quiz them. The phrases, "Does anyone have any questions?" or, "Now, what would you do next?" are good ones to use. Make sure the people you're walking through the game are actually hearing and understanding you.

If you're trying to show people to play the game, your objective isn't to win the game. In your metagame, victory is determined by how well the players understand what's happening in the game they're playing. Victory for you doesn't look like beating kittens who are playing a game but don't really know what they're doing. You're looking to turn these people into lions, at which point you can crack their skulls unrepentantly.

The Step-Up Technique

Let's say there's a game you got that you're sure your group will love, but it's a complex game. Your group isn't very familiar with this type of game or its mechanics. This is the perfect time to level up their understanding of the game by stepping them into the full version of the rules.

Think about when you've experienced or seen a run-through of a demo version of a game. Play is fast, fun, and simple, and the demo rarely encompasses all the minutiae and nuance of the game. Rather, it emphasizes the basic mechanics and why the game is fun.

To do this successfully, you need to break down more complicated games into simple versions of themselves. That may mean shrinking the game's length so players can get a full play-through of a single game in a relatively shorter time. They'll be able to learn the mechanics and strategize. I'll often reduce the number of game turns in fixed-length games, for example, to let players get a full play-through from start to end to see how people play and win.

It may mean stripping the game of the more complicated elements until the players master its basics. I may simplify the values of successful dice rolls to a single number so everyone can remember it and learn the mechanics. Or I remove entire game effects until the mechanics of the games are mastered by the players.

Teaching a game well might mean introducing its core mechanics through another game with similar but simpler mechanics. I might level up players into complicated miniature war games by introducing them to a basic miniature board game such as Ninja All-Stars (to master moving and attacking mechanics), moving them up to a boardless miniature game like X-Wing (to help them visualize and anticipate movements of their opponent), and then showing them the most complicated version of that style of game like Warmachine and Malifaux.

PLAYING THE GAME

Here's what coaching might sound like: "Before you go, let me remind you that you can do two of the following actions this turn in whatever order you choose: walk, run, shoot, and search and trade items from your backpack into your hand or with another player. Looking at the board, it might be useful to help your friends who might be opening up a big room full of zombies in the next turn. They may owe you money, but if they get killed by zombies, they'll never pay up."

Alternatively, instead of simply laying out options, play a turn. You make the moves for them as you go through the game turn, explaining the logic behind each turn. That might sound like this:

"So for this turn, if I was playing as Jane, I'd take the Flying Orc because they can go wherever they want and orcs are awesome. She'd start conquering everywhere. She'd put tokens on these territories because they're better to defend, score 5 points, and finish the turn happy. Now it's Kevin's turn, who has a couple of good choices. He'll take Diplomatic Dwarves, because they're really defensive, and conquer in this region because it's far away from everything else and will let him keep his territories longer. We'll put the dwarf tokens here, score 3 points, and nominate Dawn with his diplomatic ability, meaning she can't attack him this turn, which is useful since she's next to go. Dawn will activate her Amazons and try to take over the leftover empty territories since they're easy points. She'll score 3, and that's the turn.

"Now if nobody has questions, let's reshuffle the deck and play through the game properly."

The step-up method of teaching games works because it doesn't overwhelm players with information and focuses on mastery before moving on. It's building fundamental game skills, and sometimes you need permission to mess with the in-box rules a little for the enjoyment of all the players.

I love this technique for teaching games, and if you go about it this way, your chances for success are substantially higher than throwing your friends into the deep end and hoping they can swim.

HELP PLAYERS DEVELOP MASTERY OF COMPLEX GAMES

Some games, particularly those where players create and collect their own list of components (like miniatures, cards, or other elements that represent their force) or strategic games, typically have a higher learning curve that can be a challenge for a new player. This applies to veteran tabletop gamers as much as to those new to the hobby.

When veterans to the tabletop hobby pick up a game that's involved, mastering it takes time, advice, and encouragement. Fostering a love for a game that your friends are a part of and that you feel passionate about means you have to walk a fine line between giving guidance and not being condescending (or at least being *perceived* as condescending, which is just as bad).

Here are my tips to helping you support your love of a game and develop skills for gamers who are new to it without insulting their intelligence, making them end up angry and resentful.

Give Them Primers to Develop Their Knowledge Base

When a player is unfamiliar with the kind of force she's playing against, it helps to clarify what things she should know in order to make smart decisions. A lot of games rely on players having a knowledge base of the game as a whole. That knowledge is developed over time. You can't expect a new player to understand what the threats may be to her or to anticipate what moves may be coming—all this when she's still developing an understanding of what her own force is capable of doing. She can learn what works in her own force by playing the game and experimenting with possibilities, but she can't make strategic decisions having never developed knowledge about an opposing force.

When gaming with new players, I find that they appreciate a rundown of the kinds of threats they'll be facing from my force at the start of the game. With miniature war games, I'll go through everything I have to give them an idea of what each unit does and

TIMING IS EVERYTHING

As an example (albeit negative) of the importance of teaching others about games, I can mention an experience I had with one of my favorite miniature war games, Warmachine. The system is fantastic, but the game itself is incredibly unforgiving when players make strategic errors. To give some context, the game I was playing had a time limit of ninety minutes, with forty-five minutes allocated to each player. We timed moves with a chess clock. Serious stuff, I know. I spent a total of eight minutes deploying my force and resolving my first turn. My opponent took advantage of my strategic errors, and within ten minutes of his own clock time, he deployed his miniatures, took his first turn, and won the game by assassinating my army's caster (the force's general).

I'm not a novice to games or gaming. I'd probably not take well to being babied through play, but I didn't exactly learn much about how I could improve, what my tactical errors were, and how I could avoid that in the future, and ultimately that's what the path to mastery is. So when you're playing with someone less experienced, find a nice way of helping them gain experience.

what makes it effective. This way they have an understanding of how they can respond to that and anticipate those units working.

There is nothing that kills the enjoyment of a game faster for a new player than losing a game because he was surprised. Gotcha moments in games with new players are a sure path to destroying their love of the game quickly because it's demoralizing. Losing due to your own ignorance can be extremely dissuading. So help develop a basic understanding of whatever your players are up against so they can make better decisions.

Talk Your Own Strategic Logic Aloud As You Move

Giving new players a frame of reference, showing the kind of logic and paradigm a game uses, will help develop the right mindset for the player so he can both see how decisions are being made and how to make that work for him. It may sound like this:

"I'm going to set this unit up here so I can block your unit from charging my general. Now I'll move this unit here so I can hopefully thin down your heavy hitters with some decent shooting. And now that my shooting unit is out of the way, I have clear charge lanes for my army's battering ram."

This sort of advice gives the player an idea of the kinds of threats he's facing without sounding condescending about what he should do in his move.

Breakdown the Game after It's Over (with Permission)

If a novice gamer loses to a more experienced one (as is the case in many complex games), take the time to talk to her about the game. After a game, talking about what a player could have done to win the game or improve her play is a great way to help her get better at it. Give her props for the moves she made that made you sweat.

Before you give feedback about how she could have played better, ask if she's interested in hearing what you think she could have done to beat you. If she's amenable, talk about it with her. If she seems disgruntled or politely says she's not interested, don't push it. Sometimes losing stings a little too much, and it's too fresh. Instead, offer to talk about it when she feels like it; sometimes that's over drinks, which is a great place for conversations of this sort.

This whole business of fostering the mastery of a game comes back to facilitating its enjoyment. It means caring as much about your opponent's fun as your own. If you're personally invested in a game, both in time and in money, you know how hard it can be for new players to stay with it. So do your best to spread the love—if something brings you joy, share it rather than quashing it.

3 ESSENTIAL GAMER SOCIAL SKILLS

DON'T BE A DICK
(OR SMELL LIKE ONE)

There are certain skills that every gamer should be equipped with, many of which aren't formally outlined or taught in the context of gaming. They may have been taught on the playground to us as small children by chiding parents or teachers.

In the context of gaming with grown-up toys, however, it's easy to forget ourselves or, worse yet, let the comfort, stress, or competition related to the game affect our self-awareness.

When these skills are ignored, gaming gets uncomfortable, awkward, and unpleasant. I once played a game with one kind of dick who was impressively able to embody all of the kinds of dicks I describe in the dicks section of this chapter. This guy was moody and sulky, argumentative about every rule, beardy . . . eventually he rage-quit the game. It was a remarkable expression of dickhood, and in the end I stood there stunned at how *ballsy* he was to act like that. It wasn't a good time for anyone, and now that dick (let's just call him Richard) will forever be referenced in print by being described as a dick over and over again. Don't be Richard.

In this chapter, I'm going to talk about how both sides in a gaming argument can be at fault (to differing degrees). I'll cover why it's not always our fault as gamers and attendees that gaming stores and conventions have a smell but why it's our job to do something about it. I'll talk about how you can still be competitive while also being fun to play with, and how your intent as you approach a table will color everyone's experience—your own and everyone else's. But first, let's start with the most important rule:

HAVE FUN

This is the rule that is inherent in every game but isn't usually included in the instructions. It's easy to tell you not to be a dick, but sometimes that's easier said than done, especially when you're playing competitive games. It also happens in games where part of playing is to express frustration, menace, or antagonism to your opponents.

The guideline is simple: Have fun while facilitating fun for everyone around you. That sounds loaded—because ultimately whether or not the others you're gaming with have fun is their choice, not yours. But here's an easy way to gauge if you're doing your part: Ask yourself if you are playing in a spirit that helps fulfill the expectations of fun everyone signed up for.

When you sit around a table with other players, you're gaming with others under a (typically unspoken) social contract. It gives you permission to engage in certain behaviors, depending on the spirit of the game and the event you're playing in. The context of this contract defines everything else.

If you're casually playing with friends around your dining table, what constitutes being a dick is different than if you're playing that same game against complete strangers at a competitive tournament. In your home, name-calling and trash-talking may very well be part of the fun and completely acceptable, based on your existing relationship with these people. Denying them permission to mulligan a move would probably be a dick thing to do. Those same behaviors with strangers at a competitive event, however, would be different. In such a setting, it's wholly inappropriate to trash-talk or otherwise mock your opponents. However, it also would be considered reasonable that all the players abide strictly by the rules and thus aren't allowed free mulligans.

Don't be a dick: It's simple, but also context sensitive, so be thoughtful and be aware.

HOW TO DEAL WITH DIFFERENT KINDS OF DICKS

There are, unfortunately for the world, different ways to be a dick. Here are a few stereotypes and kinds of gamers you want to avoid being as well as avoid playing.

The Beardy Gamer

I love bearded gamers, but I hate beardy ones. If you've never encountered the term, "beardy" is a pejorative term to describe gamers who are being dicks. The term hails from the (now out-of-print) game of Warhammer Fantasy, where certain dick players would play Dwarves—the only fantasy race with guns. They'd line up on the edge of the board and shoot at their opponents, giving their foes no choice but to advance into bullets and die. Such Dwarf players became known as beardy (as Dwarfs, in addition to guns, have beards).

Those players weren't breaking any rules, but they were breaking every social contract associated with the game. There's nothing sporting about the way they played—playing a game where the outcome is already determined before the game even starts isn't fun, nor is making another human go through the motions of that wholly unpleasant experience just so the beardy player can get an ego boost.

If you encounter a beardy gamer in the wild, the best way to deal with him is to concede the game. Nothing drives him crazier than to win a game without actually going through the motions.

PLAYING THE GAME

Cassidy was playing at a casual war-gaming event and ran into Richard, who had earned himself the local honorific of Esquire because of his tendency to argue over rules. She knew that she'd be in for a fight beyond the one that would happen on the table.

At one point in the game, Richard, as per the rules of the game, deployed from reserves his own scratch-built model (one that he had cleared with the FLGS as okay to play as it was built using products from the store, and the tenor of the gaming atmosphere was that it was casual, accessible, and supportive of creative modeling) and proceeded to open all of its doors, significantly increasing the size of the model's on-table footprint (thereby taking up more space). The model pretty much took up the entire width of the table, and due to his prior clearance of using this scratch-built model as a "counts-as" model within the game, he then cited rules stating that unless Cassidy was going to attack the model, she could not move her own models within 1" of it. (Yes, the rules were written as such, but the game was never designed to have a table-spanning model.) He essentially gave himself a buffer to prevent her from moving across the table while also taking advantage of the rules allowing his own models to move through "friendly" models (which was also permitted in the rules). This essentially cut off Cassidy's ability to charge and initiate melee attacks without being limited himself. He was giving himself a significant advantage while also putting Cassidy at a significant disadvantage.

Cassidy walked away from the table rather than continuing the game, though she mentioned Richard's dickery to the staff before she left, which ultimately got Richard banned from playing in the store for six months.

Sometimes just stepping away from the table and saying, "I think you need this victory more than me" is enough to steal their "victory" from them.

The Rules Lawyer

Rules lawyers are a frustrating breed to play against. They will debate the rules of a game with you until you're exhausted.

Worse still, rules lawyers tend to focus on pedantic interpretations of English words. It shouldn't be that big a deal, I suppose, given that all game instructions are written in English. But remember, I said earlier that a lot of board game instructions have been translated, usually from German. To a rules lawyer, what would otherwise just seem like awkward or incorrect grammar is a rules-changing event of epic proportions. Rules lawyers believe that if the meaning of something isn't spelled out in triplicate, it's fair game for their endless interpretation.

Conveniently, they only argue about a rule when it benefits them—they won't correct incorrect interpretations of rules that are detrimental to their opponent.

A rules lawyer tries to bend the rules in her favor until her opponents break. While it seems the rules lawyer is trying to play by the game's rules, she's actually trying to manipulate the rules in her favor. She's cheating, or at least trying to, and that's why she's being a dick.

Rules lawyers are easily shut down if you know another— preferably simpler—interpretation of the rule in question. If there's no neutral third party who you can consult (like your FLGS staff, another player, or an event organizer), suggest that you roll a die and determine which interpretation you go with based on luck. The key is to not engage in debate. If you do, it'll never end.

The Incredible Sulk
(AKA the Rage-Quitter)

You can't easily identify this gamer when he first approaches the table; it's almost as if he's hiding in an alter ego who seems perfectly nice and fun to play with. He may remain in hiding, and usually does while he is in a winning position during a game. If, however, the table turns against him, the big green monster takes over, turning an unassuming, friendly, and perfectly normal opponent into an irrational beast.

The beast may be one of two distinct varieties, though both resemble a toddler throwing a tantrum. The first, the Sulk, may completely withdraw from the game, no longer engaging in play or trying. He pouts like a child who isn't getting exactly what he wants. He's full of self-pity because the world revolves (or should revolve) around *him.*

The Sulk may evolve (like a Pokémon) directly into the second kind of beast: the Rage-Quitter. This can happen at any point; this type of gamer gives up on the game entirely, even though there are others around the table still enjoying it. Sometimes the Rage-Quitter leaves the room in a huff, or he may sit silently at the table, making the rest of the gaming experience uncomfortable and unenjoyable for everyone. Rage-Quitters have been known to flip tables, throw dice, and generally act like a badly behaved two-year-old.

I know I keep saying such behavior is like a baby's. Handling the Sulk or Rage-Quitter is very much like handling a toddler. Sometimes you can reawaken the rational gamer within the Sulk (probably not within the Rage-Quitter). Use phrases that give him permission to opt out of the game before the tension escalates.

Politely point out the behavior is affecting others; this may pull the player out of his self-focused moment.

Give him a moment to take a grown-up timeout by asking, "Did you want to take a break and calm down?" Alternatively, I'll suggest that the player recognize that there are others around the table and that turns of fortune are part of the game by asking, "What can any of us do to make this game more enjoyable for you?" Sometimes it's better to wait until the monster retreats, and you can talk to the now mild-mannered player about how such a monster resides in him and to keep it in check.

The Sulk can do this sometimes because the player who resides within isn't aware of it. Sometimes what these players need is simply the awareness that there's a monster within that only they have the power to fight.

BE A GOOD WINNER

I used to play games when my daughter was five. She is my own flesh and blood. I carried her in my womb for ten months prior to having her extracted from my body by a team of highly skilled medical professionals. I love this human being very much. I say this because I want to contextualize the following statement: I hated playing games with her at that age because she was a *terrible winner*.

My daughter would dance around, singing gleefully, "I beeeaaat yooooouuuu!" She'd randomly remind me of her past victories in nonrelated conversations. It would be bedtime, days after we last played, and in the middle of her bedtime story she'd interject with: "Hey! Remember when I beat you at Snakes and Ladders?"

My daughter at the age of five was a terrible winner. And yet I know adults who are comparably bad at winning. Actually, when I reflect on her poor tendencies as winner, I can't really help but see myself, because I'm an especially terrible winner.

I once played a friend (and past coworker from a gaming store we worked together at) whom I hadn't played in over a decade due to geography and circumstance. In that game I acted like a total dickbag, celebrating every canny move I made with excited jumping, squealing, and even air punches.

My husband and I play competitive events together, and in one particular event for a game that I was very new at, and purely through a fluke of math and modifiers, our shared one-to-three win-loss record still had me finish higher in the standings than him. I was ecstatic, and for the next week I referred to myself within our home as, "The Superior Warmachine Player of the Household." I am the woman he married and the mother of his child, and yet for the week that behavior continued he had to remind himself why I was so awesome.

While in many cases my own outgoing and excited personality is a boon, when it comes to being a winner, I could definitely learn some restraint and empathy instead of acting gleefully unrestrained while proverbially kicking my opponent's teeth in.

1. *Don't make your opponents feel bad about losing.* You may want to play games with them again, and even though you've played better than them in at least one game, don't let that win define your relationship with them.

2. *Be grateful to your opponents for your gaming experience.* Sincerely thank them for playing and being fun opponents; it's the polite thing to do. Shake hands and acknowledge their best effort against you.

3. *Offer to play a game of their choosing in the future.* Don't be the player who only wants to play games you win. Playing games of others' choosing not only demonstrates you're a good sport, but it shows that you value the relationship you have with them, even above winning. Value people over victory, so no matter the outcome, the people you played with will choose to play with you again. Sharing food and drinks after games tends to smooth things over pretty well. (As an aside, I know for a fact that cooking my husband's favorite foods after being *oh so delightful* after the first Warmachine event we played at together did very much help him remember why he loves me.)

BE A BETTER LOSER

Sometimes a bad loss or a turn of fortune can take a player from a reasonable human being into a big, ugly, tilted monster. Sometimes tilting actually affects whether or not you can win, because your emotions get in the way of your judgment and reasoning.

So here are the basics for you to avoid being a bad loser, and possibly prevent getting slapped so hard you can taste fillings the next time you lose a game.

Recognize That *It's Just a Game*

Sometimes it feels like the stakes are higher. But when you boil it right down, the loss of a game doesn't affect your life in any significantly detrimental way. Losing a game won't cost you years of your life, your health, or the roof over your head. (If you're risking any of those things playing tabletop games, you may wish to reconsider some of the decisions you've made to get there.) Getting mad about the outcome of a game is the ultimate exercise in futility.

Congratulate the Winner and Learn from the Loss

She beat you by being better and/or luckier than you. Accepting the loss graciously is really about recognizing what you did wrong and what the winner did right, or how much more lucky she was than you. Trying to undermine the win won't make you better at the game, but recognizing what happened and how you can adjust for those conditions certainly will.

Measure the Fun You Had
Rather Than Weighing the Outcome

A fun game is one where you're enjoying it while you're playing, not after victory has been settled. Look at the experience holistically rather than reducing it to the outcome.

If you look at the game as being an experience that you may not control all of, and recognize the only thing in your control is your reaction, you can take away the best parts of the game and leave the rest on the table.

DON'T SMELL LIKE THE ELEPHANT IN THE ROOM

Let's get real about hygiene. Gamer funk is a real issue. To illustrate, check out this excerpt from an e-mail newsletter from an FLGS:

"We would like to remind all of our customers that attend our events: even though we are a Game Store, there are certain hygiene standards that are to be followed. Taking a shower, putting on some clean clothes, and wearing deodorant before attending an event should be the norm, not the exception. Those who have body odor that is offensive to either our staff, customers, or other gamers will be asked to leave and rectify the situation. This is a general reminder to all."

I once spent a summer working at a large-chain tabletop gaming retail store. On my first day of training, the orientation included hygiene expectations. I've never worked another job where that subject was part of the training.

It's my observation that gamer funk isn't completely a product of a lack of hygiene, but that gaming environments are also not generally conducive to keeping people from sweating. Gaming often happens in smaller spaces whose priority in design isn't ventilation and temperature maintenance.

Even around a kitchen table, the number of bodies sitting for hours, eating, gaming, and socializing, all the while emitting sweat and heat—well, let's just say it doesn't keep people smelling their best.

PLAYING THE GAME

The first time I attended AdeptiCon, one of the biggest miniature war-gaming events in North America, was one of the worst experiences of gamer funk I've ever lived through. I was attending the con mostly to play smaller games I didn't have the opportunity to play in my local gaming area, but I had friends playing in the team tournament, where over 250 teams of four had registered to play Warhammer 40,000, the most popular miniature war game of the time. Between my own games I went into the grand ballroom where the team tournament was being held to stop in on my friends and see how they were doing.

As I passed through the doors, the smell of the more than 1,000 gamers hit me like a ton of bricks. There was so much sweat in the air that you could feel the difference in humidity when entering the ballroom from the hallway. It was *rank*. The situation wasn't the fault of the gamers (entirely), but when you put that many people in close proximity, accompanied by poor ventilation, the smell is inevitable—and awful.

The worst part was that when I approached my friends and remarked on the smell, *they didn't notice it*. Their brains and olfactory senses had grown accustomed to it. (I'm assuming this was some sort of survival mechanism. Had they recognized how bad the room smelled, they might have quit the event.) This is why being vigilant about your surroundings and being self-aware enough to notice your own perspiration levels are pretty darned important.

There are certain things about your body you can control. Here are four rules to follow to keep the odor at bay:

1. *Shower before you hit up your gaming night or event.* This is especially important if it's going to be three or more hours. You'd be surprised how badly an entire role-playing group can smell after a late-night, six-hour marathon session. Good gaming sessions include tension and stress, and those are sweat triggers. If you start fresh, you're less likely to leave smelly.

2. *Be prepared to mask your smell as the session goes on.* A spritz of body spray or a freshening reapplication of deodorant can go a long way in making both you and your gaming colleagues more comfortable. Don't overdo it; you don't want to end up smelling like an elevator of old ladies.

3. *Dress in layers.* That poor maintenance of temperature in gaming venues mentioned earlier goes both ways. Wear your geekiest hoodie, with a T-shirt underneath. Peel layers off as appropriate (hopefully before you start sweating) and throw on a sweater if you find yourself shivering.

4. *Hydrate* with water *and avoid drinking too much alcohol.* One of the reasons at-home gaming groups can collectively pump out the funk is because they're often drinking alcohol during gaming sessions. There's a whole biological reason why alcohol makes you sweat. I won't bother spending time explaining the metabolic processes as it relates to vasodilation and sweat production since you're not here for a science lesson. But I will say that taking in

water to both stay cool and keep your blood alcohol levels low will keep the funk at bay.

Smell is a real issue when it comes to gaming, and the more effort you put into not smelling offensively, the more comfortable you and everyone around you will be. That's a good thing.

BE A GRACIOUS GUEST

Chapter 6 covers hosting your own gaming nights, but a key element to not being a dick is to be a fantastic guest when you go to someone else's house to game.

Be Helpful to Your Host

I'll be blunt; you're a grown adult. You can put your dishes in the sink or dishwasher, and you can throw away your own garbage. Believe me when I say there's nothing stopping you from helping tidy up after gaming night, including moving furniture back to where it belongs, putting the game away, and cleaning up the detritus of less gracious guests.

Ask your host if there's anything she'd like you to bring; ice, snacks, or drinks are easy to pick up. Offer to show up early to help set up. Your host may or may not take you up on the offer, but she'll appreciate it.

Also, use coasters if you're offered them. It's just good manners. Hosts who have coasters care that they're used; trust me on this.

Be on Time

A well-organized gaming night presumes everyone who shows up will be participating. Being late means you're likely delaying the game for everyone else, who are waiting on you. That means a later start, which also means a later end for your host. If you can't be on time, give your host a heads-up as soon as you know there

---

PLAYING THE GAME

I once had three gamers hang out in my hotel room and turn it into their own personal frat party. By the end of it, two of them needed me to drive them home because they were local and didn't have a hotel room, and I was married to the other one. One of the gamers had thrown up in the bathtub; another had thrown up in the sink, clogging it. Leaving chunks of poorly chewed regurgitated chicken in your host's hotel sink is the exact opposite of being a good guest. Mostly because your host will have to fish the chunks out of the sink with her bare hands in order to unclog it and avoid paying additional room charges.

---

will be a delay. If you know you're going to be late, tell your friends to start without you.

Be Mindful of Your Alcohol Intake

Gaming night should be fun and is often pretty uninhibited, but at the same time, a guest who has had too much to drink is not a good guest. For safety's sake, if you do drink, have a way home that doesn't involve driving. If your host has offered overnight accommodations because of your condition, accept. Sloppy gaming can be fun if everyone is into it, but if you slide into sloppy but nobody else is there, you can be a bit of a burden.

Keep in mind that if all the players are good visitors, the host will probably want to do this again. You may have another regular hangout for gaming (in addition to your FLGS). On the other hand, if after game night the host's house or apartment looks like

New York after the Avengers fought off Loki, he probably won't be so interested in repeating the experience.

All in all, being a good guest is about being considerate of your host and not making him do more work than he initially signed up for. He might not want to clean water rings off his table, or chunks of food out of his sink; either way, he'll appreciate your efforts.

DON'T BE TOUCHY-FEELY
WITHOUT PERMISSION

There will come a day where you're walking through your FLGS, a convention, or some other gaming situation and you'll see a game whose components are incredibly cool. So cool, in fact, that you'll feel drawn to them, and you may feel compelled to pick them up. Here's a rule to help keep your fingers from being broken by a stranger: *Do not touch game components without first asking permission.* Yes, that includes game components that aren't being played with in that moment, and it is doubly important not to touch game pieces in a game in progress.

This situation is most common to games that have components that are customized, crafted, or painted by one of the gamers. It may also come up in situations with collectible items (like cards) that you might wish to see closer.

If you'd like to see something close up, open by positively remarking on the item and ask to see it closer: "I really like the color scheme you chose. May I pick it up for a closer look?"

If the owner says no, which is her right, walk away. If she says yes, ask her how best to hold the component, as she may know any weak spots or may not want too much pressure placed on a specific spot.

Ultimately, you have to respect the game's owner. Remember your mother's advice to look with your eyes and not your hands, and you may save a significant amount of grief (and having to find finger splints at the drugstore) in the future.

LEND AND BORROW GAMES RESPONSIBLY

There's so much more to borrowing and lending games than you'd suspect. If you're borrowing and lending to a friend, it's a pretty big exercise in trust. There are a lot of upsides to borrowing games: It gives you a chance to try a game out before you commit to buy it, and if you're lending, it means your friends can get to know a game you like enough to have paid money for it. It might also get you playing with them without teaching them how to play (presumably you're lending them the instructions as well).

But this good-faith covenant has the potential for pitfalls. Here are some tactics to avoid any difficulties.

If You're the Borrower

If you're borrowing, be clear about when you intend to bring the borrowed game back—the lender should never feel like his game is just being stored on your shelf. You need to take better care of a borrowed game than your own games—returning a game in a condition that is worse than the condition it was lent out at is a huge breach of trust. So don't do that.

If you wreck a game or lose its components, you can sometimes reach out to the publisher and ask for those missing pieces. If it has them, the company will usually send them to you. If you can't get the missing or damaged pieces, don't just return the game to the owner without them. If you can, buy the game again and offer him the new copy or any of the components to replace the lost or damaged ones.

PLAYING THE GAME

Stella is a particularly generous gamer and has willingly lent out her games and rulebooks to friends to get them interested in the games she loves. Unfortunately a couple of her friends had taken advantage of her generosity and failed to return her games in a timely manner. After an uncomfortable situation where a friend kept putting her off without returning her game, Stella did a few things to help politely remind her friends to give her back what she had lent.

She started setting up calendar reminders for her friends when she'd lend anything out (some on Facebook and some as e-mail event invitations), telling her friends that they help remind her who she's lent what to while also letting technology remind people to give back her stuff. When she'd get the reminder, she'd send a follow-up message asking when her friend was free to hang out and play the game that was borrowed. If a friend didn't like it, she'd offer a chance to hang out and just take the game off his hands. It gave her a reason to hang out with her friends, play more games she loved with them, and help them learn it all in one fell swoop, while also not being overly imposing.

Stella also made a pact with a good friend, Katie, who would help her retrieve games. Theirs was a really friendly and totally unintimidating shakedown operation; Stella was the loan shark and Katie was the muscle. She'd tell the person who hadn't yet returned a game as agreed that she had offered to lend said game to Katie. She'd offer to come by herself and grab it for Katie or have Katie swing by and pick up the game. This really helped Stella avoid having awkward and confrontational conversations with her friends about returning her games.

If You're the Lender

If you're on the other end as the lender, there are a few things you'll want to do.

First, be prepared for something unforeseen to happen to your game. It's never intended, but if a game is too precious to you to contemplate something happening to it, don't lend it out. Similarly, your game may come back with all the components in the same condition, but it may not be put back in the box the way you like it and normally have it organized. Be okay with that.

Be assertive with your games. Sometimes you have to hound people who have borrowed from you to get your stuff back. If you don't have the stomach to ask for your own stuff back, you probably shouldn't lend your games out. You don't have to be a mob boss, hacking kneecaps if you don't get your stuff back, but you shouldn't be hesitant to follow up with your friends. An easy way to have that conversation is to ask your friend how she liked the game you lent her, which can lead you to telling her you need the game back as it was promised back to you.

If you're lending out your games, don't let them out into the wilderness without protection. Check out Chapter 6: Hosting Game Nights for tips on protecting your games, so you don't lose friendships over spilled milk (on your tabletop game).

PUT YOUR PHONE AWAY

Distraction not only undermines your ability to focus on a game, it effectively tells the people you're gaming with that whatever is going on elsewhere is more important than the people who are there with you right now.

It is utterly infuriating to be sitting at a table with someone and have to remind him that it's his turn to act, or constantly have to repeat what actions were taken by players prior because somebody was looking at her phone and not paying attention. There is no Facebook post, Tweet, or Cracked.com article that needs your attention more than the game you're playing right now.

To be fair, there are certain situations where that may be the case, but in most situations, unless there's a pressing reason (one that's also known to people at the gaming table) for you to check your phone for messages, just put it away. If there is something that requires your attention to the extent that you can't turn off your phone, you probably shouldn't be at a gaming night. Have a pregnant wife who might burst at any time? Stay home and play games with her. Have a call with a possible employer? It probably won't help the interview along if your friends are in the background laughing about their highly inappropriate Cards Against Humanity card combination.

You can put your phone away for games, that is, unless it's really a glamored disguise for your magic wand to help you fight He-Who-Must-Not-Be-Named. In which case, Harry, just don't let the Muggles see it.

4 HOW TO PLAY GAMES

(SO YOU DON'T GET SMACKED DOWN)

Chapter 1 covered some broad game-defining mechanics. This chapter covers the basics of game mechanics, showing you how to conduct your gameplay in a way that is both fair and fun for all involved.

It may seem like rolling dice or moving pieces is simple and straightforward. But it's not until you're in the midst of fighting about a game component's facing or arguing if a cocked die counts that you realize the importance of adhering to these basic conventions. Such things as deciding whose turn it is or what counts as a dice roll may seem straightforward enough and hard to screw up. If only that were the case. The fact of the matter is that every action listed in this chapter is a result of a gaming-night horror story (or many horror stories).

At home, follow the rules in this chapter to the letter and your games will play faster, smoother, and friendlier, and you'll have more fun. When playing games with strangers at your FLGS or at a convention or event, adhering to these rules will keep you from getting smacked down as a rude dick, or at least keep you from sitting at a table surrounded by people who are highly annoyed at you (for good reason, I assure you).

You will also have the added benefit of avoiding confusion, which sometimes precipitates rage-quitting accompanied by table flipping. Neither of those is a part of a good gaming experience.

Given that you've proven how intelligent, interesting, and attractive an individual you are—well, I mean you bought this book and read this far in it, didn't you?—I don't want you being humiliated because you counted results of dice that fell off the table onto the floor. Of course not! So let's get to it.

A QUICK NOTE ON CHEATING: DON'T

There is no game you need to win so badly that you need to cheat. The possibility of being alienated by a gaming community or being publicly outed as a cheater, particularly in the age of the Internet where your past actions have become part of a permanent record, accessible by all, is too much. If you don't believe me, just look up the names on Fantasy Flight Games Suspended Participant List on Google. Now imagine what a potential employer, a possible gaming partner, or a blind date who Googles those names would think. It's just a game—you can afford the loss.

ROLL YOUR DICE THE RIGHT WAY

If you've presumed that rolling dice is a simple task, I'm so happy for you. You have never encountered a douche dice roller, which is something you never want to do. But just in case you don't want to ever *become* a douche dice roller, here are the rules to dice rolling.

If you're rolling dice as a game action, announce that action. If the action has a variable number of dice rolled, announce how many dice you'll be rolling and how you derived that number. Many games (especially D&D) have different kinds of dice that are rolled in different situations. Announce which of these you're rolling (for instance, "I'm rolling a d10 for Initiative").

Then roll the dice.

If you need to pick up the dice to roll again, let your opponent see the dice you will be rerolling first. In one game I play (Warhammer 40K), you roll a mitt full of dice and then get to reroll the dice that are higher than a certain number. I roll, remove any misses so my opponents can see that the dice I'll be picking up again to reroll are actually qualified to be rerolled, and then reroll them. Making a comment about what number you're looking for ("Anything but ones!" or "Three plus is what I need to hit") also makes it clear what you need so your opponent has the chance to point out misses. I've seen douche dice rollers who pick up their rerolls first, don't let their opponents inspect the dice results before they start rerolling, and are unclear about the number of dice they're rolling, let alone how they derived that number.

Another thing that is in extremely poor form is to throw dice forcefully, knocking over gaming tokens, components, or other elements of the game—sometimes knocking them right off the table. This is especially douchey when components are hand-painted or fragile—a forcefully thrown die can mar a paint job or damage a model. If you have ever done this, let me explain some basic physics to you: Rolling dice harder doesn't make them roll higher. Believe me when I say that's the kind of behavior that will make you unwelcome in some gaming circles in the future, with good reason.

If you're rolling a handful of dice and you drop one (or it escapes your hands for whatever reason), consider it rolled. Don't wait to read its outcome before deciding to pick it up and reroll it. That's bad form. If there's confusion whether the die actually rolled (giving it the opportunity to change its result) or it just fell flat, ask your opponents if they'd prefer you to reroll it or not. You have to pay for your clumsiness by submitting to their wishes.

Cocked dice can also put people on edge. Cocked dice are dice that do not land flat on the playing surface. This is common when you're playing on a gaming surface that is uneven because various gaming components are part of the play surface (for example, when you're playing with miniatures laid out on gaming terrain). If you have a second die that is the same size, you can balance it on top of the cocked one. If the second die doesn't balance, reroll it. If you don't have a second die to check, just reroll the die (after, of course, you ask all of your opponents if you can reroll it because it is cocked).

Some games (such as tabletop war games and role-playing games) don't include dice in the box and allow you to bring your

ON DICE TRAYS

You should consider getting a dice tray, which will help with a few of the issues I point out when it comes to dice rolling. Companies like Wyrmwood make luxury ones, and many FLGSs sell standard ones; if you don't want to purchase one, you can make your own. In the past I've used shoebox lids, gift boxes, and picture frames (with the glass removed, of course). Anything with a lip that has a flat surface for dice to settle flat and that won't dominate the playing surface makes a good dice tray.

own dice to the game. Do not, under any circumstances, think that novelty image dice are appropriate when other people need to see the outcomes. If a reasonable human being cannot read the result on your dice from six feet away, get better dice.

Oh, and one more thing: Dice that land on the floor need to be rerolled. Floor dice don't count if you're playing a tabletop game, *capisce*?

FOLLOW TURN SEQUENCE

Some games have a very simple turn sequence that is easy to follow. Some games have complicated turn sequences, with many steps and processes, upkeeps and new costs, and other nuanced mechanics.

Those games tend to have gaming aids that help walk players through all the steps and show in which order they're to be taken. Follow the turn sequence as laid out in the rules; don't try to do things out of sequence as it tends to change the balance and fairness of the game. If you do, it's easy for other players to accuse you of cheating, especially if you're trying to get benefits, such as revenue, before you are allowed to. Cooking the game this way could then allow you to purchase upgrades or abilities that should be out of your reach. (In Robo Rally, game sequence is crucial, especially the order in which game effects happen. Going out of sequence in this case directly affects the outcome of the game.)

When you're going through your own turn sequence as a player, just announce which part of the turn you're at. Let's say you're playing a game that has an upkeep phase, an action phase, and a housekeeping phase. Announce those as you go through your turn. Saying, "For my upkeep phase I'm going to . . ." is an easy way to make it clear to your opponents what you're doing and why you're doing it.

If you make a mistake during one of your phases, stop and ask your opponents if it's okay for you to correct what should have happened in an earlier phase. In particular, if your correction impacts your opponents negatively, always ask permission before you go back to make the correction.

Only Ask for One Do-Over

When it comes to asking to correct mistakes that negatively impact your opponents, only ask to correct one type of mistake once. After that, you should eat your mistake because you didn't learn from the first time when they gave you leeway. Trust me: once you have to eat a mistake that costs you a game win, you'll never make that mistake again. Think of it as getting a learning opportunity rather than screwing yourself over (although you've done both).

If the mistake negatively impacts you, offer to correct it the first time. After that, if you make the same mistake again, just correct it and tell your opponents why you're not following the turn sequence in that moment and that the outcome will benefit them as it hinders you. Again, think of it as a teaching moment for yourself. At the same time, be forgiving and understanding to others when it comes to do-overs (remember to value the relationship over the game).

TRADE CORRECTLY AND POLITELY

As a mechanic, trading components allow players to try to get what they need to win a game; the other side of it is that the trade may benefit another player and help their strategies to win the game.

If this mechanic is allowed by the game, make sure you know what the window is for negotiating trades. Sometimes it's only done in a particular phase of a turn, sometimes it's done in between turns, and sometimes negotiating trades can be done anytime during the game.

For example, in Zombicide, players can trade equipment and items, and virtually all trades positively impact the group, since the game is cooperative. Within the game, trades are an action a player takes during her own activation, meaning it takes up one of that player's available actions during that activation. Despite the cooperative nature, out-of-sequence trades not only affect the flow of the game (as they can confuse whose turn it is to activate, or worse yet, disrupt the active player's turn) but also basically

NEGOTIATION AS PART OF GAMEPLAY

In the popular board game Diplomacy, there's actually a phase of gameplay called the diplomatic phase. During this time, players can talk to one another and negotiate strategic alliances, treaties, and so on. But—and here's the big thing—negotiation *only* happens during that phase of the game. Anyone trying to do it later or earlier in gameplay is, well, a douche.

cheat all the players around the table from a well-earned victory; out-of-sequence trades are essentially cheating against the rules.

Some players may also want to know who's trading what, as that will affect their strategies. If the rules are not explicit about how trades should be handled, decide by consensus (preferably before you start playing the game) whether or not the group wants trades to happen one at a time so everyone can know what's happening between players or if multiple negotiations can happen simultaneously.

Negotiating trades can interrupt game flow, and even the negotiation of a trade can impact the gaming experience of all the players, whether or not the trade goes through. Of course you want to win and make trades beneficial to yourself, but also remember that there are other people sitting around your gaming table. Be considerate of them and the time they are spending watching other players negotiate and deliberate. It's not the most exciting thing in the world.

For this reason, brevity when negotiating and executing trades is hugely important and considerate to all your opponents. On the flip side, don't monopolize game time by hesitating on a trade offer you already made. Worse still is asking to reverse a trade that was done according to the rules. Only children under the age of ten may ask for a trade back; otherwise, you're stuck with the trade you made, because you're a grownup. If you made a mistake in offering or taking a trade that was bad for you, you gotta eat it. That's part of the game.

Trading with these things in mind will keep things fair and keep the game moving. And that's a key element to good gaming experiences.

SHUFFLE AND DRAW RESPONSIBLY

Playing with cards is a staple in the world of tabletop gaming. Sometimes you're actually playing a card game (e.g., Magic: The Gathering or Vampire: The Eternal Struggle), and sometimes the cards are an important part of the game, along with other components (e.g., Ticket to Ride or Sid Meier's Civilization: The Board Game).

If there are cards involved in a game and there's a shuffle-and-draw mechanic, shuffle your own deck but offer your opponent the opportunity to cut the deck before you draw. This is particularly polite if you're playing a collectible card game, and each of you has her own deck.

Furthermore, only draw the number of cards you are permitted as outlined in the rules. If you draw more cards and the procedure for handling such situations isn't outlined in the rules, announce to your opponent that you've unintentionally drawn too many, and offer to shuffle the surplus cards you've drawn back into your deck. Also offer to allow your opponent to cut the deck again. If he agrees or offers a different solution that is amenable to you, go with that. The key is to be clear and open about what you're doing with your deck.

SCORE AND CALCULATE POINTS PROPERLY

Games have various ways of gaining points and tracking score. You should be clear about how you're scoring. Like every other aspect of playing games, it's far better to overcommunicate than undercommunicate. If you do the former, you're just an overly meticulous gamer. If you do the latter, you might end up getting labeled as a cheater, particularly if you mess up on the math more than once.

This is especially true if you're the player who takes the role of the banker or something equivalent within a game. You want to

---

PLAYING THE GAME

Here's how Mika announced her scoring: "I control X, Y and Z, which gives me 3 points, and I won battles in A, B and C, which gives me 5 points. So I'm up 8 points and need 8 tokens."

Mika's fellow players appreciate the clarity her announcement brings. It leaves no ambiguity in their minds about how she's earned the points she says she scored.

Contrast that with Sean: "I scored 8. Gimme 8 tokens."

Apart from being rude, there is no clarity how those points were scored, so for all Sean's opponents know, he could be fabricating a number. That's fine if Sean is playing with trusted friends, but it's a douche move if he's playing pickup games in his FLGS or something more competitive.

BE HELPFUL WITH SCORING

If your opponents are articulating their points like you, and you see an error, feel free to be helpful and redo the points tally with them, especially when they're cheating themselves out of points. Remember: you want to win these games legitimately, not because you were better at math than your opponents. Victories that come from math errors are hollow at best.

be seen as the person who just is sitting closest to the tokens, not as the person who might be embezzling under everyone's noses. Don't be *that gamer*.

If scoring is done in a specific phase of the game, announce the score you've earned in that phase as you track your score.

Announcing the way you're scoring also has the added bonus of giving your opponents a chance to correct you if your math is off or if there are points you're missing. Ambiguity is the enemy of decisive victory, so be unambiguous as to how you crushed your opponents' skulls and earned points with their blood.

BE DECISIVE—BUT BE POLITE

There's nothing more annoying than playing a game with a player who takes forever to take his game action. Don't be that guy; be decisive, announce your action so everyone knows what you're doing, and then take it. If you want a mulligan on an action, ask all of your opponents, and make sure they agree it's okay. If it's a casual game, it should be fine. Just don't do it often because it's poor form.

Hemming and hawing over your options, being ambiguous about what actions you're going to take so that nobody actually knows what you did in your turn, or constantly taking an action then reversing your decision only to take another is rude and annoying. It slows down the game to the point that players may get bored and walk away from the table.

If you're the player who hems and haws when you've had everyone else's turn to plan what you're going to do, you're taking too long.

It's pretty forgivable if you don't know the game, but if this is the third time in recent memory you've played it, you should have it down. If you're the kind of player whose friends are always mocking you for taking forever, here are some tips to help you improve your decisiveness and speed:

- If you're a deliberate player who takes time to think out decisions but commits to them, make a concerted effort to deliberate faster. Anticipate the play as it unfolds, and start limiting your options as your turn to act nears so you have fewer options available to you. Use a small timer to help manage your own time so those around you know you're also sticking to it and can hold you accountable for it.

- If you're an indecisive gamer who continually questions your next move, just commit. Again, a timer may help you make a decision, so the decision you make when the timer dings is the one you're stuck with. The best way to learn a game is to make mistakes as you go. Through your mistakes you'll be able to measure the effectiveness of strategies.

Time is a factor when playing games, so don't hog all of it when your turn comes around. The upside is if you play quickly, you'll probably be able to sneak in another game or two, which is a darned sweet deal.

HANDLE SIMULTANEOUS REVEALS RESPONSIBLY

Sometimes a single action needs to be taken by all players at the same time. For example, in Sushi Go! players draft cards for their sushi platter. These are scored at the end of the turn, where drafted cards are revealed at the same time as hands go around the table. In other games, there may be voting, revealing, or claiming actions. No matter the action, the simplest way to do it is to prepare your action, have a player count to three, and on three have all players take their single action.

The countdown ensures that a simultaneous reveal is truly simultaneous. If you don't have a person to own the countdown, this simple mechanic turns into a hot mess fast.

If the reveal goes sideways for whatever reason (for example, a player didn't have an action to reveal and missed out on the reveal entirely), you can redo the turn, but everyone involved gets to pick a new reveal and do it all over again. If you can, reset the turn back as far as you can. That may mean resetting the game turn partially or fully and possibly redealing cards to players.

As always when it comes to playing fair, everyone but the offending player gets a say in how far back you go with the game. Choose the option that satisfies the most. That way nobody feels unfairly picked on or disadvantaged, and you'll nip drama and table-flipping anger in the bud.

MOVE YOUR TOKENS THE RIGHT WAY

In games where movement matters, the precision of execution, measurement, and facing make a huge difference in the outcome. (This is very much the case in miniature war gaming.) Thus moving your models in a way that is fair will keep accusations of unfair play to a minimum, quashing any gaming-night drama llamas.

Where movement matters, learn the rules for measurement first. Some games allow for premeasuring before moving; some games require anticipating and estimating where the token will end up. If you don't know what's allowed in the game you're playing, look it up.

As when taking actions, it's best to announce your movement. Announce which token is activating and what move action (if there are different ones available) it will be taking. Then measure it.

- If you're using a template for movement, hold the model steady first, press the movement template into the token, and steady the template. Then lift the model and move it.
- If you're using a tape measure, steady the tape measure over a part of the model and measure from that point to the end of the tape measure. Move the model, not the tape measure.
- If you're moving a token a set number of spaces on the board, as you move through a space, count up until you reach the maximum number of spaces you're allowed to move through.

Once you've completed your movement, announce that it's done. Be clear to avoid confusion.

When measuring, measure to the same point on the model when you're first starting and finishing the move. That way you don't get any extra movement. When in doubt, presume a model is always out of range rather than in range for whatever it needs to do (that way you don't lose friends over a disagreement about one-sixteenth of an inch of movement).

Games that rely on movement depend on precision. Practice moving your models so you can visualize the movement and you know how to manage your hands. Turns out that moving one hand while keeping the other one perfectly still takes some practice. It also takes practice to not knock over other things while moving your models. There's no faster way to a bad reputation at a gaming table than to cheat on your movement and knock models over while you do it. So don't.

5 GAMING GROUPS

KEEPING YOUR PARTY FROM KILLING YOU

One thing that sets gaming apart from other geeky hobbies is that tabletop gaming requires you to share the same space, oxygen, and experiences with another human (or a group of other humans). Because gaming necessitates social interaction, having a regular group makes gaming easier.

Moreover, the culture of gaming is very much about community. This makes your gaming group much like an adopted family. You play together, you fight each other, you die together, and you put away your toys together. That's why you really want to make sure that your gaming group meshes well. No matter how quirky each of you are, as a group you should all get along and enjoy being together. You only have so many hours you can give yourself the gift of leisure—you don't want to be spending it with jerks.

My own gaming group, while full of crazy characters, is like family. We're so close that we can survive one of us slapping the other across the face and still want to hang out and be friends. That kind of friendship, forged because of gaming, is only possible because we mesh and because in the end we're thoughtful of each other.

And that's especially important when you have one player whose dice are so bad he's pretty much a gaming group's nemesis in any RPG scenario. (In case you were wondering, it's Nathan. It's always Nathan.)

Here are some guidelines to help you keep your gaming family healthy and functional.

TREAT YOUR GROUP SORT OF LIKE YOU'RE DATING

There's a certain dynamic within gaming groups—every person brings a unique element. You meet people, you regularly hang out, and you generally like being in each other's company. Like dating, there are a few rules to follow.

Be Open to New Experiences

When you're going out on a date with someone you like you may do things out of your comfort zone, like eat weird cheeses or go to a bar you only know by reputation. In those cases, the person you're with matters more than the food or the venue. Same goes for your gaming group: You may never have played a certain game or tried a genre of game, but if you like the people you're hanging with on gaming night, it's worth the effort and the risk.

Do Not Bring Old Baggage or Drama to the Table

Nothing ruins a date faster than when you let old relationship baggage surface during your date. Same goes for gaming nights and ex-gaming groups. Yes, that player may remind you of someone you used to game with whom you hated, or someone else may be friends with people whom you didn't like at your FLGS. And sure, you may have had some pretty traumatic experiences playing Power Grid. But that's in the past. Growing beyond those experiences is why you're out gaming with new people. Don't let that drama and baggage keep you from having a good time.

Be Yourself, but Be Your Best Self

Don't pretend to be somebody you're not—faking a personality or being inauthentic to try to impress other people is the direct path to being unhappy and making others unhappy with you. That said, be your best self—the self who follows reasonable gaming and social etiquette (as we've covered so far), is thoughtful and considerate of others, and is genial and positive enough for people to want to be around.

Pay for Food, at Least for the First Night

If you're coming into a new gaming group, bring something to eat. Low blood sugar is the enemy of fun games, and as humans, we bond over food and eating together (it's also why first dates often involve meals). So bring some easy-to-eat baked goods like cookies, splurge for pizza during a break, or grab a veggie and dip tray and share with your newfound gaming group. This small gesture not only shows thoughtfulness but will make it easier for you to feel more at home with your new group.

Whether you're joining a gaming group or gaining a new person, remember that you're all checking each other out, figuring out if you'll all be fun to game with. So be open, be yourself, and be genial, and let your gaming night play out.

JOIN OR START PICKUP GAMING GROUPS

So you know how to behave yourself when you're in a gaming group, but how do you find one? The starting point, as you might have guessed, is your FLGS. After all, that's where people like you hang out. Here are some things you can do to meet people and get them to sit down and play a game with you.

Be Active in Your FLGS's Community

Your FLGS might host a weekly or monthly gaming night for a particular game or host an event around a specific game. Those are great ways to find people who like the games you already like—in other words, people with whom you already have something in common. A lot of people turn their regular gaming night at their local FLGS into a loosely affiliated gaming group. When the FLGS changes its gaming night schedule, usually the people who regularly meet on those nights then organize themselves as a gaming group.

You can also ask around at your FLGS, and sometimes the staff can put you in touch with people who organize games.

If there is no gaming night or gaming group, you can talk to your FLGS if you want to start your own as well, which is a great way to both meet people and spread the love you might have for a game (for more about hobby championing, see Chapter 11).

Look at LFG (Looking for Group) Postings at Your FLGS

Some FLGSs have community bulletin boards where people can put up announcements. A group looking for additional players or players looking to join groups or start groups will probably post there. These listings usually focus on long-term campaign games (like role-playing games or campaign-oriented tabletop games).

Some FLGSs even have websites, forums, or even a Facebook group that allow people to look for and find gaming groups for various games as well as organize groups. Just another service provided to you by your FLGS.

PLAYING THE GAME

If you want to post an announcement, here are examples of what it should look like:

Experienced and easygoing player looking to start a Pathfinder group. Looking for an experienced DM and 2–4 additional players (no experience required). Able to host on Tuesday, Wednesday, or Saturday nights. E-mail yycpathfinder@gmail.com—let's make this happen!

Let's fly casual together! X-Wing Miniatures Game players wanted to start a campaign-style gaming night. Have some homebrew campaign rules to see who can control Endor! Rebel scum and Imperial players welcome. Meet new players, play on your own schedule, report your battle outcomes, and see who ends up on top! Join the Facebook group YYC X-Wing for details and to enlist!

The postings read a little bit like dating profiles mixed with wanted ads, describing the personality of the gamers as well as the kinds of games they're looking to play and what days of the week work best.

If your FLGS doesn't have a bulletin board, suggest to the staff they get one—it's always good to have a community board in a community hub, after all.

Look for Groups Online

There are so many ways to meet gamers online; each different city has a preferred platform. Facebook, Meetup.com, and even Craigslist have postings for groups who regularly meet to play specific games. Just remember basic safety protocol when you're looking to meet up with strangers on the Internet. Meet up first in a public place (like your FLGS), get to know each other (and feel free to bail if you get weird vibes), and tell friends where you are going.

You can also start your own Meetup or group. Again, you know you're not a murderer, but for the safety of all, including yourself, consider hosting the first few games in a public venue so you can all get to meet each other before letting strangers into your home.

AVOID GROUP DRAMA

When you take a group of individuals and you put them into a social group, it doesn't matter how nice, friendly, genial, or otherwise cohesive they are—there will be disagreements. Personalities clash, disagreements happen, and competition complicates and amplifies everything. Following are a few rules to avoid gaming group drama:

Set Some Ground Rules

Know that there will be disagreements. If you're starting your own gaming club or regular event, it's important to set ground rules for a group to start. Be clear about the expectations for the group. They may be cultural (like how it's not cool to complain about losing) and/or procedural (what to do in the event of a rules disagreement). Sometimes anticipating the most common causes of disagreements (both in and out of the game) can help keep drama from starting.

Having a list of basic gaming etiquette for everyone to follow is a good idea. Make sure you have many copies of it to share with everyone in the group.

Let the Small Stuff Go

Not every decision will go your way. In cases where things aren't as you'd like to have them, sometimes you've just got to accept it. Complaining openly without any suggestions to improve the situation doesn't help anyone, and dwelling on things that are in the past and can't be changed is an exercise in futility.

As a Disney princess once sang, let it go.

Direct Actionable Feedback Appropriately

Sometimes if you have a legitimate complaint, it's something that can be fixed. If it's something to do with the group's organization, talk to the organizer. Be prepared to propose something to make things better for everyone, not just you.

Telling everyone but the person who can actually do something about the problem isn't the right way to go about fixing it. You can't hope someone will take the torch from your hands and run with it. If it's serious enough to precipitate a change, put your big-kid pants on and say something. If it's not, refer to the previously discussed point about small stuff and letting go.

Don't Involve Yourself in Gossip

Talking about people disparagingly behind their backs is extremely rude behavior. Worse still is participating in gossip about that person and spreading those untruths as if they were fact. That's just asking for drama, which you don't need in your life.

Being complicit as someone gossips is just as bad. Standing idly by in situations of gossip makes you an accessory to it. Sometimes you just have to say, "Hey, that's not cool. If you're going to keep going, I've got to walk away." Whether those around you change their behavior or you have to change your location, at least you can be smug in being above gossip.

Don't Be a Douchebag Online

One of the worst places for drama is social media. Be thoughtful in the things you post, and remember that the previous points in this section apply as much to your online interactions as they do offline. Gossiping, passive-aggressive complaining, whining about the small issues, and ignoring your group's rules while online is just asking for trouble.

So is starting big fights with people online. If you have a disagreement with someone in your group, handle it face-to-face. A lot of people grow virtual spines when they get online and start saying things they'd never in a million years say to your face. Don't be like them.

Know How to Apologize

Sometimes it happens: You act like a total dick. Maybe you lost your cool at the table; maybe you got caught up in some weird gossip. Maybe you did something you didn't mean to do, and someone took it personally.

Owning your part in whatever happened and being a bigger person is sometimes the only way to make things right. Offer a sincere apology, and buy the person you've wronged a coffee or a beer in good spirit. Face whatever consequences that may come out of the situation.

Sometimes a sincere apology and the promise of changed behavior goes a long way to avoid explosive drama.

When it comes to addressing drama, you can only do as much as all the parties involved are willing to do. In the best-case scenario, relationships can be mended, but sometimes the only thing you can do is control your own actions and provide sincere apologies and authentic promises of changed behavior. Ideally, though, everyone is following these rules and not doing anything, intentionally or unintentionally, to upset anyone in your group.

BE GOOD AT BREAKING UP

Sometimes personalities clash. Sometimes as you get to know the dynamics within a group, it becomes evident that certain individuals are as useful and positive as a turd in a punchbowl. Maybe they're bad losers or terrible winners. Maybe they're Incredible Sulks or rules lawyers. Maybe they're just gossipy Gladyses. They've been warned, over and over. They've promised to change but haven't delivered.

If it's your group, it's up to you to handle it. Sometimes you have to break up with a player on behalf of your group, for the sake of the group. If you don't know how to break up with someone and haven't mastered the "It's not me, it's you" line, then you'll appreciate this section. In an ideal world, you'd never need this stuff, but we all know how imperfect this world is. Here are some steps to follow if things come to a point where breaking up is all you can do.

Give the Player a Chance to Change

Talk to the player and give him an informal verbal warning before any specific disciplinary action is taken. Talk to the player about what he's specifically doing that is detracting from the fun of the rest of the group—don't blame, but just talk about what can be done moving forward.

Write Things Down

If you've given an informal warning and the player hasn't followed it, sometimes a written warning outlining behavioral expectations will make things clear. You can also outline consequences if the player has another infraction. Consider suggesting the problem player take a break from the group to give everybody some cooling-off time. Sometimes distance makes things better.

PLAYING THE GAME

Is there a nice way to tell someone to stop being a dick? Yes. I've had this type of uncomfortable conversation with folks in the past, which seems uncomfortable but is really just a casual conversation. Here's what the conversation looked like:

"So Kevin, we've noticed that you've tended to raise your voice at whomever you're playing whenever you're losing the game. I understand, as I've felt those same things you've felt hundreds of times over. I know you know as much as I do that your opponents don't want to make you mad, and they don't control your dice. I know you're a good person and can help keep this place positive, so I'm going to ask you to help us here and just be more aware of how you talk to everyone else, and stop yelling at people, even when the game isn't going your way. Do you think you can do that?"

The point is to have people recognize problematic behavior while not being confrontational. What helps make the conversation easier and more palatable is that it expresses empathy and understanding, and it invites the person to join in with the rest of the group rather than isolating the offender for her poor behavior. People respond better to that kind of feedback than one full of blame, which just breeds resentment.

Sometimes Breakups Are Good

If a player continues to behave poorly and makes the gaming experience worse for other players, it's time to break up. By this point you've moved past discussion. Sometimes the conversation is as simple as, "This isn't working. I'm sorry but we can't continue gaming with you."

Sometimes a player may decide that the group isn't the right fit for him and chooses to no longer participate after having either a verbal or written warning.

However the breakup goes down, breaking up with a player isn't a comfortable situation, but the discomfort of it is significantly less than the discomfort of gaming with someone who is undermining the group's fun.

6 HOSTING GAME NIGHTS

YOUR MARTHA STEWART LARP ADVENTURE

Live-action role-playing (LARP) as the homemaking host or hostess may seem like a daunting task, but hosting gaming night is a fantastic opportunity to share gaming with friends into the early morning hours, without worrying about how late your FLGS stays open or how to get home on public transit.

The rules in this chapter are intended to help you get through a night unscathed, without having harm done to your home, your games, or your friendships. Grab an apron, skip the casserole, and get rolling.

A QUICK NOTE ON INVITATIONS

When inviting people over to your hosted game night, be clear about the arrival time and when dice will start rolling. Be clear about what games will be played, if that's settled, or if your guests should bring a game to share. Let people know ahead of time if they need to bring something (whether that be dice or food) so they don't show up unprepared.

PLAN THE RIGHT KIND OF
GAMING NIGHT

When hosting a game night, the key rule is to do things that make hosting enjoyable for you rather than stressful. If you're not having fun at your own gaming night, there's a serious problem. Sometimes having a structure to a gaming night makes it easier to host, especially since you can know what you need to do to make it happen.

Following are ideas to help structure your own gaming night:

The Game Potluck

Everyone who is able brings a game to share and play. You can set up several different tables to play the various games on. People mix and mingle throughout the night. Break the night out into a few sections so games should wrap up around the same time and people can try other games. Feel free to also ask guests to bring something to eat, to go with the potluck theme.

The Theme Night

You give your guests a theme for the evening, which is mirrored in both the food and games. A zombie-themed game night is great for Halloween, with games like Zombie Dice and Zombicide on the game menu and undead Halloween treats and eats for the food portion. Similarly, a Japanese-themed night might include games like Sushi Go!, Machi Koro, and King of Tokyo with sushi, noodles, and sake served for noshing.

The Campaign Night

If you're hosting a campaign in your home (whether RPG or some other kind), having a sustainable schedule and manageable task list for yourself is the key to success for longevity. Keep a set schedule if regular gaming is going to occur weekly or monthly. Have people come an hour before to eat and set up, and have the game start rolling at a regular time, with a regular end time. Building predictability into the schedule and making preparations beforehand makes RPG nights fit into people's lives, not just for the players or DMs, but also for you as the host.

The Party Game Night

This is a great structure if you're looking to have a small house party that also includes gaming, because many tabletop games don't support more than six players. Spend an evening playing a number of games that are relatively short, have high replayability, and support large numbers. This gives natural breaks for people to see to their needs, mingle, and nibble on the food, and it gives people a chance to step out from playing without impacting the other people present who want to play.

No matter how you structure your game night, you want to make sure that you are able to enjoy yourself as much as your guests.

PROTECT YOUR FRIENDSHIPS BY PROTECTING YOUR GAMES

I love the feel of a new board game. There's always an excitement, quickly tempered by having to pop out what feels like an infinite number of tokens, markers, and other accessories from their cardboard sheets.

And then there's the twenty-plus-page rulebook that you have to read.

While tiresome, there is no better way to show your games love than to take the time to protect them. Games are a significant investment—even small-box games that easily fit in a pocket or purse can cost upward of $30.

Games are the things you're more likely to want to pass down to future generations rather than destroy by loving them too much. In terms of assets, the value of my tabletop gaming collection easily exceeds the value of my car (and will probably be better appreciated in forty years' time).

Yes, paper and cardboard will eventually deteriorate, but there are ways to slow that and fortify your games against the act of being handled, played, and even flipped (it happens).

There are a few things you'll want to have on hand when you first crack open a modern board game:

- Card sleeves in appropriate sizes
- Rubber bands or hair elastics (I favor hair elastics because they're gentler on cards)

- Snack- and sandwich-sized ziptop bags
- Small binder clips or paper clips
- Matte spray lacquer (optional)

Most if not all the items listed should be available at your FLGS, craft store, or dollar store.

Because we handle cards and our hands are covered in natural oils and moisture, they break down first, so sleeving them substantially increases their longevity.

Most cards are standard sizes, like phone-charging cables. Further, most games will tell you on the back of the box what size of cards are contained inside, making it easy to buy appropriately sized card sleeves. The most common size of cards is standard size—the size of cards for collectible card games like Magic: The Gathering. There are also standard and mini-sized card sleeves for European games and American games, as well as oversized cards, referred to as tarot-sized.

Even if your card sleeve doesn't fit perfectly, you're better off with cards that are inside sleeves than ones that are not. There's no board game police who will come knocking at your door because you decided to put your mini cards into standard card sleeves since that's what you had on hand. You can always get better-fitting ones later.

In many games, cards are separated into different uses; this is where your elastics and clips come in. Separate out the cards by their groupings and bind them together using either an elastic band if there are handfuls of cards or clips if there are just a few. This not only helps keep your box organized but helps make setup of future games a lot faster.

WHEN ACCIDENTS HAPPEN

Sometimes things happen to our beloved board games. Components get lost, boards get damaged, accidents happen. In situations like this, the first thing to do is reach out to the game publisher. If the game is still in print, many publishers will happily send replacement components for their games that have been lost or damaged, often for free.

All those pushed-out tokens need a home, and that's what the ziptop bags are for. Sometimes games include bags, sometimes they don't, so having some on hand is always a good idea. Again, separate the tokens by their uses within the game for easier future game setup.

If you have a large board, game tiles, or other cardboard components you want to protect, give them a spray with some matte spray lacquer—I prefer Testors Spray Lacquer Dullcote. One or two thin coats won't affect the look of the board, but it will provide some protection from drops of liquid, greasy fingers, and the occasional wipe down, which is always a good thing.

A good host is always prepared. Paper towels should always be at the ready in case something gets knocked over or spilled. If any paper components get wet, dry them as best as possible. Sticky, sugary drinks can typically be sopped up initially, and then the sticky residue that remains can be wiped away with a baby wipe (I'll get to the importance of them later). Wood and plastic components are generally easily wiped or washed.

With all that said, don't expect to be able to pick up the game where you left off. Picking up the game board and pulling off game pieces to protect them will disrupt the game so much that you may have to reset the game or start a different game if it's later into the evening.

A spilled drink doesn't have to be a catastrophe if it's dealt with immediately. Just don't expect to be able to go back in time when it comes to playing the game from when the drink was spilled.

CONSIDER YOUR GAMING SPACE
AND FURNISHINGS

A good host considers how many guests she'll have and prepares for that number, whether that's for a dinner party where you have to figure out how much shrimp to serve or a gaming night where you need to know how many chairs and how big a table you'll need.

The rule is simple. Make sure each person has a reasonable amount of space to play the game around your table. There should be room for the gaming components that each person will be playing with without anyone encroaching on another player's space.

The amount of room will differ from game to game. Some games for four can be played with as little space as the seat of a chair. Another game may require more space than a dining room table for six.

Pick the game you'll be playing and lay it out on the table, leaving space for each player to manage his or her player components. See how it feels—the only way to know if everything will be comfortable is to see for yourself. You may realize you need to put the leaf in your table or that you'll need to get a couple of plywood boards to put on top of the table and increase the gaming area.

You may also realize everything is fine, in which case, hooray!

Similarly, if you're hosting a party game night, make sure there's a reasonable amount of furniture for at least half of your guests to sit on and there's enough room for your guests to play the games you've selected for the evening. You can presume reasonably that some invitees will not show up, and others will be mingling about or playing games in various states of standing, sitting, or laying on the floor, like Werewolf (in which the dead lie, the living sit, and the moderator stands) or Two Rooms and a Boom (where people are standing and moving between two rooms—the perfect house-party game.)

Look around and account for your gaming night needs in terms of space and furnishings—nothing is more of a party downer than having planned to play a game and realizing that there isn't enough room to play it.

SERVE FOOD AND DRINK WHILE AVOIDING DISASTER

There are two fundamental truths that require food to be present at gaming nights. The first is that low blood sugar makes it impossible to have the most fun you can have, and the second is that we as humans share food to develop cooperative bonds (read: friendship).

But there's also the undeniable fact that food can be damaging to games, and preparing food for an entire gaming night may seem overwhelming. Here are the basic rules to ensure food doesn't end up damaging your games, and possibly your friendships.

If It Needs Utensils, Eat It Before Game Time

If it requires a vessel and utensils to eat, it's not food to be eaten during a game. Similarly, if it's greasy, leaky, saucy, crumby, or otherwise messy, it is not fit for consumption while gaming.

Don't Feel Compelled to Supply All the Food

Organize with attendees to share snacks that everyone can bring. This isn't some 1950s dinner party, where you're expected to shake martinis and slave in the kitchen for hours as a host. It's perfectly reasonable to host a gaming night with food provided in a potluck style. After all, you're still doing the dishes.

Limit the Food That Is Consumed and Available During Game Time

Leave out a small selection of game-friendly snackable food. This is where 1950s homemaker skills really can pay off—great snacks for games usually come in the form of veggie sticks. Other great options include cookies and pretzels. You'll notice all these foods are easily handled, are not greasy, and also run the gamut of snacking preferences—healthy, sweet, and salty.

Big Gulps Are Better Than Wine Glasses

So here's the straight fact: Tippy glasses filled with colored drinks that stain are a surefire way to heartbreak on gaming night. They will inevitably ruin your games. Lidded drinks with stable bases, on the other hand, are a safe choice.

Water is the preferred liquid consumable for gaming night (both because it doesn't induce sweating like alcohol and because it's clear). Sometimes, of course, having something with caffeine or alcohol just makes gaming night better. Think about serving fancy water or fizzy soda water. Throw a few cranberries and slices of citrus or cucumber into a jug of water so your guests have a

ON BABY WIPES

Baby wipes are an excellent thing to have on hand for gaming night, even though you may not have a baby. They can wipe up sticky or greasy fingers, let you give a quick wipe to the table before laying down your game, and they pick up little crumbs or small spills before they turn into big things. Buy a box and keep it handy—I swear you'll use it.

few options apart from soda or alcohol. Serve in heavy-bottomed glasses that are hard to knock over.

Have Breaks

Taking regular formal breaks between games or during a game to see to personal needs allows people to grab something more substantial to eat or drink if they need it or go to the bathroom. Formalizing time for self-care during gaming night will help the group's overall stamina for gaming as well as allow people to still enjoy the munchies they want without destroying your games or feeling as though they're interrupting play.

As humans, we've evolved to bond with each other over the sharing of food. But those bonds are easily shattered when the food destroys a $90 game. You want to do everything you can to avoid that, and that sometimes includes being thoughtfully restrictive about the kinds of food and drink available.

ASSESS YOUR SUCCESS

After the dust has settled on your successfully hosted gaming night, reach out to your guests to make sure they had a good time. It's also a good idea to get a feel for what your guests thought of the games that were played. If a game is really popular, it might be a hint that you should invest in expansions. If a game isn't so well received, find out what didn't work. It'll help you make better decisions about games to play in the future. It's completely appropriate to ask your guests if they had a good time so that you can ensure the next gaming night goes off without a hitch.

Doing this postevent work gives you the opportunity to assess the experience of hosting so that you can address any issues, if any came up. Touching base with your guests in this manner gives you a structured conversation that also lets them touch base with you. They can tell you if someone had a little too much to drink or if they might have forgotten something at your place. Sweaters, dice, and even Tupperware have been left at gaming nights. It helps folks rest easy to know that it's being taken care of.

Make sure you give yourself the space and permission to figure out how you can make hosting easier. Assess what worked for you and where you can ask for help—a good host knows that sometimes you can't do everything yourself.

It can be extremely gratifying to host gaming events. Having your friends game in the comfort of your home can be the best experience ever, provided you focus on keeping it enjoyable for all involved, including you.

PLAYING THE GAME

There are a pile of easy ways to see how your gaming night went. Sending individual notes by e-mail or posting a single thank-you message on Facebook (tagging all the attendees with some fun (and hopefully not-so-embarrassing) photos of the night's events are an easy way to touch base with everyone and get a feel for what everyone thought. Even responding to your initial Facebook post with a, "So, what was the best game everyone played? I noticed there were a lot of people playing X. Was it good?" Questions like that also spark conversation and debate, which gives you a sense of who liked what and why. If you keep the tone of the messages on the casual and conversational side, rather than sending out a Google form sheet with yes/no answers, you'll probably get more honest, candid, and sincere answers as well as a better response rate. Sure, it's less formal, but when you're measuring the quality of people's experiences, formality can be hindering. Someone who doesn't hit the "Like" button or leave an enthusiastic reply is saying something as much as people who use the "Love" button and like every comment in the thread about the night. Or they don't use Facebook, in which case, just shoot them an e-mail thanking them for coming.

7

GAMING WITH FAMILY

GAME LIKE THE BRADY BUNCH

Family game night seems like such a cultural mainstay. So why do we dread it when we're visiting family over the holidays and someone pulls an old, dusty copy of Monopoly out from a cupboard (other than the fact that Monopoly sucks, that is)?

There's a really strange mixture when you game with your family. Atop the standard competition, you may be layering years of relationship baggage, generational and cultural expectations, and humans (of all ages) whom you have to love even though they're acting like children.

Family game night success is predicated on a few things, which you'll learn about in the following sections. As with every gaming experience, the point is to help ensure everyone around the table cares about everyone else's experience as much as their own.

MAKE GAMES WORK FOR ALL AGES

The best part about playing games as a family is that there's a mix of ages and experiences in play. It means that games you're accustomed to playing (and winning) a certain way may be dramatically different and offer you and others a new gaming experience. Here are some ways to make games work for the range of ages that may be gathered around the family gaming table.

Play Cooperative Games

These games are excellent in getting a family to work together. They also help prevent competition that would alienate younger or older members of the family. Be mindful when playing cooperative games that everyone is making decisions and isn't being told what to do by a ringleader. Cooperative games include role-playing games and some board games, such as Pandemic and its expansions.

Play Age-Appropriate Games That Are Fun for Older Gamers

Here's a secret: A lot of games that are marketed for kids and found in the family section of your FLGS are great for adults, too. Games like Machi Koro, Sushi Go!, and Zany Penguins have simple mechanics but are enjoyable for all ages.

Divide the Family Into Teams

One way to help ease the age and experience gaps is by playing in teams. It helps engage inexperienced, younger, or older players to jump into a family activity they might otherwise be hesitant to participate in. Just don't have any hesitation about learning from a family member younger than you.

Pull Out Those Small-Box Games

Small-box games, because of their small size and short play time, are generally light gaming experiences that are fun and friendly. Games like Sushi Go!, Love Letter, Coup, and Zany Penguins have accessible themes that are easy to teach, pick up, and play.

Play Games with a Higher Luck and Moderate Skill Factor

Games that rely purely on luck can be boring, and so too can strategy-heavy games if you've got the wrong mix of people. You need to have a group of like-minded gamers who all enjoy that type of game to enjoy games of pure luck, or are willing to learn and play deeply strategic ones. The latter is rare, given that family gaming often includes significant age differences as well as experience levels. But games that require moderate skill in order to navigate high-luck elements are engaging for people of all ages. Everyone has a chance to win, but those with skill always have a better chance.

PLAY NICELY EVEN WITH NONGAMERS

Sometimes your gaming partners are playing with you only (or largely) because they share your bed or your bank account. Or sometimes it's because it's Thanksgiving and you all have to be in the same room anyway. Whatever. Be nice. It's worth it in these situations—it helps to pass the time in an enjoyable way as well as forestalling possibly awkward conversations that revolve around when you're going to get married/have kids/have more kids.

The key is to select games that are fun and distracting but accessible. You may even convert a nongamer into a gamer. Here are basic rules for picking games for nongamers.

1. *Avoid games with lengthy rules.* If a game's rules more closely resemble a book than a sheet, it's probably too complex to try to explain and too lengthy to be enjoyable for the nongamers in the group. Instead choose a game whose rules can be explained briefly and easily.

2. *Pick a game whose theme is audience-appropriate.* Some games are great to play over drinks with friends. Depending on your family, they may also be great games to play at Christmas or Thanksgiving. Or . . . they may crash and burn. Cards Against Humanity might be a fantastic game for nongamers who are irreverent in their sense of humor. Or it might change the way your family looks at you forever. Same goes for games whose art is risqué or controversial (I'm thinking about Exploding Kittens). Be mindful

of the sensibilities of the nongamers before you pull out a game that might be considered too crass for grandma.

3. *Find games that have mainstream analogs.* Most hardcore nongamers have probably played *something* at some point. They don't find games that are similar to familiar games to be intimidating, so use the "It's like *X*" method of teaching. Machi Koro is like Monopoly, Tsuro is like Sorry, Bananagrams is like Scrabble, and Dixit is like Pictionary. These analogies make the game more accessible and might help in both teaching the game and making it engaging by making it feel more familiar.

Ultimately the goal in playing with nongamers is to play games that are engaging, interesting, and immersive enough for them to become gamers for as long as they're playing. If you're successful in this, you might have also birthed a gamer yourself, which is always a good thing.

BE NICE TO YOUR SIGNIFICANT OTHER

This might be the most important rule in this book because it can significantly impact a lot of other aspects of your life. I cannot stress this point enough: When you play games, be nice to your significant other.

I'm going to be completely honest: I am a terrible follower of this rule, and it has led to rage-quitting on my husband's part, as well as table flipping. I know intimately what the consequences are when you're not nice to your significant other when gaming. I'm going to list a few things you shouldn't do, but trust me: I've done all of them.

- Actively frustrate or block your significant other's next move, because you know him well enough to anticipate it
- Try to eliminate her early in the game because you recognize she's your biggest competition
- Encourage others to make moves that are moderately beneficial to you
- Willingly take actions that sabotage your significant other's efforts, even though they also undermine your own efforts in the game
- Take away the joy of his victory by suggesting you're not playing to the best of your abilities

Some of these things might be fun for me (or, at least, in the moment I might *think* they'd be fun), but it really isn't fun for my husband. He likes to win. It's a super dick move of me to do any of those things.

Here's the real secret to being nice to your significant other: Care about her or his enjoyment of the game more than your own.

Being nice to your significant other means different things to different people. It means knowing him, recognizing how he likes to play, and supporting that. If you don't know what that might look like (because he hasn't told you either through words, actions, or both), here are a few easy guidelines you can refer to.

1. *Be an ally to your significant other.* That may mean avoiding direct confrontation with your significant other on the board where you can. It may also mean that in all games that have player elimination, you have to wait until you're the last two standing in the end before the gloves come off.

2. *Don't actively undermine your significant other.* Especially don't do it when you have other choices in the game. This is a super dick move and in some relationships grounds to be stuck sleeping on the couch. Let's avoid that, shall we?

3. *Be a good loser.* When he wins, be gracious so you don't take away from his victory. You should be the person your significant other can celebrate his victories with. So be nice, and maybe you'll get some special treatment because he's in a good mood.

4. *In bluffing games, always believe your significant other.* It's better to be wrong than to have to face your partner and tell her you don't believe her when she's telling the truth. It can be a Pandora's box of relationship trust issues that

you're opening. Remember the story of Devon and Kim from the Introduction? It can be like that.

There are cases, of course, in which these guidelines might not mean anything because your significant other wants you to bring it on. That's cool, too. The parameters of a relationship should be defined by the people involved in it, not by somebody writing an etiquette book. If you have a chance, talk about how each of you likes to play games and what you enjoy about playing them—that way you can cater to each other's needs.

One other thing about gaming with your significant other is that when there are others involved, you don't want your relationship issues to play out during the game. It gets super awkward for all involved. If the two of you are having a tough day, it might mean skipping gaming night with your friends. Or it might mean leaving early so as not to weigh down the gaming night of others with weird emotional baggage.

You should value the relationship you have over any game you play.

BE NICE (BUT NOT TOO NICE) TO YOUR KIDS

Playing with kids is a good thing. But you have to walk a thin line between fostering a love of gaming and quashing one.

Kids learn through play. Critical thinking, creative problem-solving, strategy, and anticipation are all skills that kids acquire through tabletop gaming. They also can develop math, reading, and spatial skills, not to mention resiliency, cooperation, and communication. They'll hopefully also learn gaming etiquette, like how to be a good winner, that dice that have fallen on the floor don't count, and that gaming means being thoughtful of others. Unless of course, you don't model that behavior. So don't be a dick to the children.

When it comes to games that have a strategic element that they're learning to master, help your kids develop those skills by rewarding smart choices. Consider handicapping yourself by limiting your own choices and the actions you're willing to take. Do this to give the child you're playing with a chance of winning without just handing the game to her.

I consider myself a victory slot machine—sometimes a child playing with me will get a payout of a victory to keep him playing. He doesn't have to win every time—it's a good way to teach him to be a good loser, to practice the game and to keep trying.

Let me be clear: You don't want to be the grownup who makes kids cry when you play with them. Fostering a love of gaming is different than fostering a love of winning. Remember the rules to help make games accessible to people of all ages, and be willing to play games that are fun for everyone.

When a child, particularly your own, beats you legitimately, the feeling of admiration and pride (for your part in shaping that child to be a savvy gamer) will ease the sting of defeat pretty quickly.

8 TABLETOP ROLE-PLAYING GAME BASICS

PLAYING PRETEND LIKE A PRO

Tabletop role-playing (also known as pen-and-paper role-playing) is probably one of the richest gaming experiences you can partake in. It helps cement relationships by giving you a reason to regularly come together with friends, gives you a common goal, provides memorable experiences, and lets you make mistakes together.

It's also one of the most accessible ways to game with friends because initial costs are quite low (there are many free and low-cost games available both in print and digital formats). After you've settled on what you want to play and have a copy of the rules, all you need is some paper, some pencils, and some dice (easily available at your FLGS).

Conceivably, for the cost of a fancy steamed-milk coffee each, you and your friends can have the needed supplies to play a campaign that can last hundreds of hours, which in the grand scale of entertainment is a hell of a bang for your buck. (Some games have gone on for years, surviving changes in players, DMs, and rule systems.)

Moreover, there is nothing quite comparable to role-playing games. The experience is immersive, action-filled, and self-determining in that you and your friends help create your own story. Even when playing through a prebuilt campaign, one that

ON DUNGEON MASTERS

For those of you unfamiliar with role-playing games, you'll probably come across the term *dungeon master* (DM), sometimes called game master (GM). These aren't players; rather, the DM or GM plays the role of a facilitator of the adventure. The DM tells you what's going on. She also role-plays the people and creatures you encounter, warns you of the challenges you face, explains the adversaries you must defeat, and brings you the gods who gift you with their blessing. If you have a DM who is good, count your lucky stars. If not, you will need one to play your games. There's a section on DMing in this chapter (with advice for a novice DM) as well as in Chapter 11: Being a Hobby Champion (with additional advice for a more seasoned DM).

may have been played by hundreds of other role-playing groups, the unique personalities of your players, as well as how you play your characters, makes for a singular experience that wholly belongs to you and your group.

If you're interested in seeing what role-playing is about, Geek & Sundry (http://geekandsundry.com) has a show called Critical Role that I highly recommend. In the show a group of actors role-play together. Watching them is both entertaining and informative as the show is exemplary of great role-playing.

I always recommend to new gamers that they try their hands at pen-and-paper RPGs because it can be such a special experience. This chapter is a resource to make that experience as enjoyable as it can be for you and your group.

GET THE MOST FROM YOUR RPG

Tabletop role-playing games are story-based games played in a setting determined by a DM (either from a published module or of the DM's own creation) where the gameplay takes place in the imagination of the players. Players create characters of different races, abilities (often determined by a die roll), and ethical perspectives (called an alignment). As the game progresses, the players describe how the characters they've created act or react within that world. RPGs have formalized rules (often quite extensive) that factor a character's skill along with chance to determine the success or failure of a character's particular action. Whether that action is successful or not is typically decided by dice rolls.

The most recognizable role-playing games are Dungeons & Dragons (or D&D, currently in its fifth edition as of this writing and nearly forty years old) and Pathfinder, a system that closely resembles D&D as it was in its revised third edition. Both games have created vast worlds in which players can adventure.

YOU AND YOUR DICE

Role-playing gamers use certain common abbreviation, including ones for dice. A ten-sided die, for example, is a d10; a six-sided die is a d6, and so on. Another useful abbreviation to know is NPC, which stands for nonplayer character. This is any character who appears in the story and is role-played by the DM.

As fun as it can be to run characters whose natures and motivations clash and conflict (such interactions make for great character development), the fact of the matter is that ultimately everyone in your group is always working toward the same goal. The vast majority of RPGs are shared *cooperative* experiences. The fun for the group (which includes the other party members and your DM) is directly related to how well you get along with each other. Value the relationships over the in-game outcomes, and remember the rest of the rules in this book, because if you're gaming for the long haul with the same bunch of people (most campaigns last longer than celebrity marriages), getting along makes everything so much easier.

In order to get the best experience when playing RPGs, there are a few basic rules you need to know:

Buy an RPG Set in a Universe That Captures Your Imagination

Here's the truth: The rules don't matter if the universe isn't interesting or exciting to you. There are RPG systems for virtually every genre, as well as for nearly every popular franchise (including Star Wars, Firefly, Lord of the Rings, and Doctor Who). If there's a particular universe that you and your group are intimately familiar with and would love to play pretend in, that's the one you should pick, not the one that seems popular or most talked about. If elves, dwarves, and dragons don't do it for your group, don't buy an RPG set in a fantasy universe, even though it's the one that is most popular.

Get the Right Dice for Your RPG System

The most popular systems of RPGs use a d20 to test for success and a variety of other dice to resolve damage and character leveling. Read your rulebook before buying your dice or anything else. It should have a list of what supplies and dice you and your party will need in order to get playing. You don't want to end up with a horde of d20s when what you needed were d6s.

Anything Is Possible

The fact of the matter is that if you can reasonably describe your character doing something, and how he would do it, it's likely that the DM will allow it.

PLAYING THE GAME

Imagine a group is playing that includes Regina (the DM) and Roger, one of the players.

Roger: Okay, my fighter leaps up the stairs to engage the ogre standing at the top.

Regina: The stairs are slippery with the blood of the spiders the ogre has just slain. What's your Dexterity?

Roger: 11.

Regina: Okay, make a Dex check for me. Roll a d20.

Roger: Rolled an 8.

Regina: Your Dexterity score increases that by 1. You make it up the stairs, but you slip on the way, and the ogre gets an extra attack against you.

Roger: Cool!

CRITS!

Many systems have in place a way for players to make critical fails and successes. Typically these rolls can't be modified up or down with skill stats as they represent outstanding success or abysmal failure.

Use your imagination and be descriptive. The more detailed you are with your actions, the more plausible an action may seem to your DM. That, in turn, may lower the success value for any difficulty for tests you need to make. Speaking of which . . .

Difficulty Is Relative in RPGs

When you start RPGing, you describe an action your character is taking. Sometimes your DM will interject, asking you to make a test for success (typically a dice roll). Basic activities (like walking somewhere or running) are presumed so easy you can do them without testing for success. In most RPGs, these tests are dice rolls.

Slightly harder actions like walking up some slightly slippery steps may require a test, but success is significantly more likely than not, unless your character has a flaw that makes him, her, or it clumsy. Don't get irritated by these tests (sometimes called "checks"). The DM is just making sure your character can really do what you think he can do.

The better your character's statistics (covered later in this chapter), the greater the chance of increasing your roll. If your Dexterity modifies your roll by 3 and you're trying to beat a 5 Dex check, you only need to roll a 2 or more on the die to be successful.

(Of course, if your character is clumsy, he may have a modifier that subtracts 1 from the die result, so you'd need a 6. See how it works?)

The more difficult the action your character is taking (picking a lock, doing an acrobatic somersault jump into combat, intimidating a grizzled bartender who has seen it all), the less likely success is and the higher a value you'll need to roll.

Have Fun with It

Sometimes the best part of playing an RPG isn't being successful, getting the loot, or saving the day. It might instead be the moment where you accidentally deafened your friend's character in one ear because you miscast a spell, or when you brought your friends to tears with laughter after playing your dim-witted barbarian as a punch-wizard trying to explain to the weakling scholar how to cast his signature spell, head smash.

The best moments in campaigns aren't just the epic victories; they're also the small moments where the game, your imagination, and the collective suspended disbelief of those in the room make the scene come alive, and those become the things you remember.

MAKE A PLAYABLE CHARACTER

Whether you're new to RPGs or you're a role-playing veteran, a key element to your fun and enjoyment (as well as that of those around you) is how playable your character is. Character stats aside, being able to pin down your character's motivations and articulate her actions and reactions will make your own playing experience both engaging for yourself as well as immersive and fun for your party.

It's thus very important to any role-player that she creates a character that is intuitive for her to play but is also interesting, engaging, and has room to grow and develop. Here are things you want to think about when you create your character.

Who Are You Basing This Character On?

It's easier to role-play a character when you have a frame of reference. It doesn't matter who you pick as your character's starting point for her personality, just that it's intuitive and straightforward for you to refer to and remember. Some suggestions:

- Think of an iconic fictional character and use that as a foundation for your character. Batman as a vengeance-seeking paladin makes sense, as does a warrior-class character based off of Wolverine. Constructing a character with something concrete in mind gives you room to envision how those characters would react in various situations.

In this way you can role-play your character's reactions easier.

- Be an exaggerated version of yourself. Try to play a heroic, virtuous version of you, or maybe an evil-twin version of you. It's easy to use you as a template and emphasize aspects of yourself to frame a character that is intuitive to play.
- Be someone you love or hate. Got a boss whom you'd love to play as a dull barbarian lout or cowardly sorcerer? Role-play him!

How Will You Incorporate His Stats Into the Way You Play Him?

A character's statistics may have an effect on how you choose to play him. A lower Intelligence score may mean your character may not be very logical, though he may still be charming. A lower Charisma score doesn't always mean a shy character; it may instead translate to someone who is just bad at interacting with people positively. The character may be rude, socially awkward, or someone who makes others uncomfortable by peppering innuendo into every conversation. (As an example, television's Gregory House obviously has a low Charisma score, but no one ever accused him of being shy.)

When you think about stats for a character, don't just play your character obviously. Make it fun for you (and everyone else) by doing something interesting that fits your character's stats and background story. A low intelligence character can be played in many ways, including as a naive childlike monk, a barbarian who only knows which end of an axe to hold, or a high charisma bard who thinks himself a rhymer but can't rhyme anything with the word *song*. Feel free to think outside the box.

What Might Make Exploring This Character Interesting?

Each character should have an element of intrigue, a secret motivation, or some sort of backstory that you and your DM can explore at a later date. You don't have to hash it out by yourself, but having a few character quirks supported by an interesting backstory that isn't obvious will give you the opportunity to explore those story hooks.

For example, not everyone will know your character has a secret phobia about dogs. Your DM should know and may use it by exposing you to some cuddly little puppies and revealing the phobia to your party. That, in turn, might lead to you hunting down the werewolf pack that slaughtered your family when you were young.

You want an interesting and intuitive character that is fun to role-play, because you're going to be spending untold hours as this character interacting with the other characters in the game. Rolling dice to resolve combat actions is one thing, but the real interactions within a particular RPG universe are done outside of combat. That's when the thought you put into your character during its creation will really pay off.

PLAY PRETEND WELL—THREE RULES FOR EVERY RPG PLAYER

One of the keys to enjoying the role-playing experience is having improvisational skills. Being able to react and respond in character in relation to other characters is the basis of improv. It's essential to playing pretend well; doing so helps scenes within your adventure advance. Solo tabletop RPGs are unpopular for a reason: Interacting with the other player characters and the DM are as much a part of the role-playing experience as battling monsters. These sorts of interactions mean being able to think on your feet; you have to be open to some zany antics every once in a while, but that's half the fun.

Being a great improviser means being a role-player who is fun to play with. So here are rules to keep you focused on being the kind of group member others will brag about.

Accept the Reality Set Before You

The DM sets the framework of the world for you. Your party members are a part of the world. The world is likely full of adversaries you'll eventually have to fight, but there's no point in fighting the world itself. Arguing with your DM about the world that is constructed for you is not only frustrating for the other players around the table, but it also gets away from the part of role-playing that is *play*. Instead, it stalls the momentum of the adventure.

If your DM describes an orc adversary as pink, despite the fact that you *know* they're green, there is no point in arguing. Just roll with the world set before you and keep the adventure going. Don't

---

PLAYING THE GAME

Imagine that you've been asked to defeat a slaver who has been abducting locals. You can stab him, free the enslaved locals, and go back to town for a reward. But that is just going through the motions and treating an adventure for justice as a fetch quest.

Think of an alternative way to add some spice while still accomplishing the objective. Maybe you capture the slaver and bring him back to the townspeople to face justice in a uniquely befitting manner. Or instead maybe you bring back his decapitated head on a pike and spike it into the ground in the town square for all the townspeople to see. What you do depends in large part on how you're role-playing your character. Each of these options is a way to inject your character into the story and have him become an element in the world.

---

try to paint the world as you wish it to be. You never know—maybe the pink orc indicates a spell a wizard cast on your party to make you colorblind to greens.

Not arguing also means not stalling play by refusing to make decisions about what you and your party should do. If you have a leader, follow her decisively. Just like when playing any other game, when it comes time to take your action, be decisive and act rather than hem and haw about what your move will be. It's better to be brash than boring in an RPG.

Add to and Interact with the World

Instead of fighting and denying the world you are adventuring in, add to it and interact with it. Talk to nonplayer characters

(NPCs) played by your DM, investigate the road less taken, and use your character to make your mark in the world you're exploring. Don't just be a character who passes through it.

It can be very easy to get caught up in simply accomplishing tasks and achieving objectives when playing an RPG, particularly if the story feels linear. But use your actions to help tell the story of your adventure. Taking the extra time may yield more interesting options and take you down new paths.

Try to Make It Fun

Sometimes on gaming night you may not be focused. Or perhaps your dice are continually rolling so low, so your character is as useful to the rest of the party as a fish's bicycle. Sometimes things aren't much fun for you in that moment. Every experienced RPGer has been there.

In those games and moments, it's really important to focus on not detracting or ruining the experience of those you are gaming with. Concern yourself instead with trying to enrich their experience, whether that's focusing less on combat and more on interacting with (and possibly antagonizing) their characters or characterizing your poor luck in entertaining ways. When you have a run of bad luck, don't withdraw from the game. Bringing attention to your personal (rather than your character's) misery breaks the suspension of disbelief. Instead, go deeper into the game and channel your disappointment in your dice into some awesome characterization to help keep the other players focused on the game rather than their friend-turned-Sulk sitting at the table.

For example, given a spiral of bad luck, your character might get irrationally superstitious, at least until she sees her luck return. It's funny to imagine and role-play a low Intelligence character trying all sorts of wacky remedies (like licking toads or becoming vegan) to lift a perceived curse.

That sounds a whole lot better than just playing Candy Crush on your phone (which you shouldn't have out anyway).

Use your imagination to become *more* immersed and *more* invested in the story of your character and your group. You'll be surprised how much that investment will pay off in fun.

KEEPING THE BAND TOGETHER: THREE RULES TO KEEP THE ADVENTURE INTERESTING

Keeping a group of adventurers, each with his or her own motivations for adventuring, focused and working in unison toward the same goal can be a bit of a challenge, though role-playing through those character differences can be fun.

With that said, here are a few rules to follow so that even though your group might not be the most harmonious, you can still move the adventure forward.

Have a Leader

The leader decides what paths your adventure will take. He may ask for advice from the party, but ultimately the decision should be his.

There may not be any reason for your group to have a specific leader. It certainly doesn't have to be some democratic decision—the leader might be the person whose character is the most charismatic or the most power hungry. The reason doesn't matter, but having a leader will help you make decisions so your group stays together on your adventure and all players have the opportunity to interact in a given situation. Branching off into individual adventures is a quick path to disengaging the other players.

Be Willing to Role-Play Interesting Party Dynamics

An amoral thief and a morally righteous cleric walk into a tavern. That's not the beginning of a joke; it's the beginning of an adventure. It sets up a relationship that will be fun to role-play for gaming session after gaming session.

Interesting party dynamics can mean playing out different party dynamics because of polar opposite perspectives. Two people might play characters whose alignments are similar but who egg each other on to raising the stakes. Playing a character with two fighters who have a strange rivalry when it comes to equipment might be a fun element to role-play. Characters spending money on impractically large swords or trying to convince each other that theirs is the superior pair of boots, set of armor,

ON CHARACTER ALIGNMENTS

Some games offer alignment options for characters, which help shape the motivations of characters and gives you a sense of how to play them. The most common alignment system is one that describes a character as existing on an axis of society's values (Lawful, Neutral, and Chaotic) as well as an axis of the character's own internal morality (Good, Neutral, and Evil.)

For example, Superman would be classified as Lawful Good, Batman as Chaotic Good, Lex Luthor as Lawful Evil, and the Joker as Chaotic Evil. There are some really fun and interesting pop culture alignment grids online using characters from virtually every fandom that you can use to help find your character's compass.

or headband might mean role-playing high-stakes games of rock-paper-scissors.

Take the time to figure out how your character feels about each of the other characters in the party and work out, through role-play, how that manifests in their interactions. It's a fun way to keep the relationships interesting.

Evolve

Your character's stats aren't static, so you should expect her perspectives and personality to change as well.

Your character may have a phobia of cats but may get saved midcombat by the druid who turned into a panther to kill all the foes surrounding you. This might be a pivotal moment for your character and how she looks at cats and druids.

If you treat your character as a fixed point rather than an evolving part of the story, you rob yourself of the opportunity to change and find her place within the group. Evolving your character so she works better (however that looks) as a member of the party is a key part of having fun and being a good party member.

Role-playing is best done in groups. If you can work within the party dynamics, you and those in your party will have a substantially more enjoyable time.

BEING A GREAT
(ALTHOUGH NOVICE) DM

Every dungeon master starts somewhere.

It used to be the case that virtually all DMs started as players and eventually became DMs as they grew in confidence and knowledge. That's no longer the case. With the explosion of interest in RPGs and entire groups taking on a new RPG, someone—even someone inexperienced—needs to step up to be the DM. There are a lot of resources out there now for DMs who are brand new. If you want to DM for your friends and you and they are new to RPGing, watch Critical Role role-play videos at Geek & Sundry (http://geekandsundry.com) or listen to the *Acquisitions Incorporated* podcast at Dungeons & Dragons (dnd.wizards.com). No

---

PLAYING THE GAME

In a game you're running, Ron, who's playing a cleric, says he wants to make a Perception check while in a cave with running water. As DM, you know there's nothing in there to perceive.

You: Okay. Roll a d20.

Ron: Fine. I rolled a 12.

You: You hear the noise of the running water echoing off the cave walls.

Ron: That's what you told us when we first entered.

You: Right.

Ron (to the others): Okay. Nothing to see here. Let's move along.

matter where you learn how to DM, the fundamentals of facilitating a good game will help ensure that all your players will enjoy the experience of playing in your dungeon.

Avoid Saying No to Your Players

Sometimes your players may describe an action they'd like to take, but you know that it's either impossible or a very, very bad idea. Here's my advice: Don't say no.

Let your players make mistakes, but make sure there are consequences to bad ideas and actions. Instead of saying, "You can't do that," let them play out the scenario and deal with what happens.

PLAYING THE GAME

You: As you're sitting by the campfire, you hear a rustling in the bushes, accompanied by a low growl. The next minute, a very angry bear bursts from the shrubbery and rushes at you.

Maria: My character steps toward the bear and falls in front of it.

You: Uh, why?

Maria: I'm playing dead so it'll go away.

You: What's your character's Wisdom stat?

Maria: 4.

You: Ooookay! You fall in front of the bear. The huge creature bends down and sinks its teeth into your arm. Roll for damage.

Maria: Crap!!

Janet: I fire my crossbow. (Rolls die.) All right! A natural 20!

You: Your crossbow bolt strikes the bear in its throat. It gasps, claws the air for a moment, and drops dead.

See how much better and more exciting that scenario is than if you'd just told Maria, "You can't do that action"?

Similarly, if a player decides to do something exceedingly stupid, describe the consequences. But avoid telling her she can't take the action she wants.

Just remember all actions are possible—some outcomes may be neutral, some may be negative. You're facilitating an experience that is a sandbox set in a collective imagination so support creativity and experimentation in that space.

Don't Feel Like You Have to Know Everything

As DM, you are like the god of the world. You are the ground beneath the players, the air above them, the nonplayer characters (NPCs) who dispatch them on quests, and the foes they fight. You are everything, and that bears a heavy responsibility.

You may feel like you need to know how every mechanic works and what every rule is, but that is patently false. What you do need to know is how to figure out a way to address situations fairly within the confines of the game. The rules support the gaming experience; making that experience fun for the players is your first priority.

You are not expected to have an encyclopedic knowledge of the game. Sometimes if you can't find a way to address an unconventional situation, and a cursory scan of the rulebook yields no support, don't hold up the game to find an answer. Instead, make it up in a way that feels intuitive and fair. You can always go back later and do a more thorough investigation on how to handle such situations, but in the moment keep the game moving forward.

Which brings us to the final point:

Don't Stick to the Rules When They Don't Feel Intuitive

If you want to reward players for great role-playing but the rules don't allow you to do so, feel free to bend or break the rules to facilitate the fun.

As DM you should be fair to your players while doing your best to apply the spirit of the rules to the game. Be sparing with your rule breaking (after all, the rules are there for a reason), but remember, facilitation is your job. The confines of the game set

---

PLAYING THE GAME

In one game I was playing in, we were fighting a group of kobolds (for the fantasy uninitiated, kobolds are lizard people—very nasty in large numbers). The group's druid turned into a bear and killed one of the kobolds with a critical hit—in fact, he chomped the little bastard in half. He then described how he wished to try to intimidate the remaining kobolds in the combat by sitting up on his haunches, letting out a loud roar, and shaking his head to cover his enemies in the blood and viscera of the eviscerated enemy.

The rules of the game don't allow for intimidation actions midcombat, but given the exceptionally well-described action, combined with the typically cowardly nature of kobolds, the DM decided to allow it. He asked the player for a roll, which he passed. The remaining kobolds ran for the hills.

The DM in that moment chose to prioritize the gaming experience over the rules. Ultimately that choice improved the experience, and that's the goal. Feel free to modify, ignore, or use the rules as you see fit to make the adventure the focus rather than the rulebook.

---

boundaries so that you are the god of the game rather than your players.

Whether you're a novice DM or have years of experience, you want to be able to walk out of a session with your head held high and smiles on the faces of everyone in the room (including yours). Have fun with your world and be fair to your players, and they'll be able to appreciate you as the DM. The last thing you want is to be the DM whose tires got slashed by his players because he wasn't fun or fair.

9 ATTENDING CONVENTIONS

GAMING WITH THOUSANDS OF YOUR CLOSEST FRIENDS

If you get serious about hobby gaming, at some point you'll probably find yourself having the wonderful experience of attending a gaming convention. It may be a small local convention or it may be a vast convention such as Gen Con or ComicCon. Within the walls of a convention center (or something smaller) you will have the opportunity to buy limited-edition or con-exclusive gaming expansions, play games competitively, meet new people, and try some great games.

Surviving conventions and making the most of them for you and for other attendees requires a very specific approach. There's so much more to it than just showing up, spending money, and rolling dice. You may be faced with dilemmas that you'd never considered: gracefully declining friends who ask you to buy stuff for them, having to cope with postcon illness, or even figuring out how to play at conventions with total strangers (though many gaming conventions are covered in a previous chapter).

Within this chapter, I'll give you the rules to convention survival.

CONVENTIONS TO CHECK OUT

There are a number of great gaming conventions to check out in the United States. Here are a few of them:

AdeptiCon: Held in the spring (late March/early April) in the Chicago region, AdeptiCon is the largest tabletop war-gaming convention, with a growing board game component. The con features twenty-four-hour gaming for many miniature war games as well as board games. While hosting events for virtually every major tabletop miniature game, it also boasts the largest Warhammer 40K event on the continent (the team tournament attracts approximately 1,000 players year after year). The Crystal Brush Awards are considered the pinnacle awards for sculpting and painting on the North American continent.

Origins: Both a consumer and trade show, Origins Game Fair in Columbus occurs in May and is put on by the Game Manufacturers Association (GAMA). It allows game publishers to show off their newest games and expansions, as well as offers opportunities for fans to play and celebrate their games.

Gen Con: Gen Con, hosted in August in Indianapolis, is a true celebration of tabletop gaming. There's a large variety of representation for gaming publishers: from Wizards of the Coast and Fantasy Flight to indie publishers the likes of GCT Studios (who make Bushido and Rise of the Kage) either as vendors or in gaming events.

PAX: PAX (Penny Arcade Expo) has gotten so big that it now has three events over the year in the United States plus one event in Australia. In the winter, PAX South is hosted in San Antonio, PAX East is held in Boston in the spring, and PAX West (previously known as PAX Prime) is held in Seattle in the fall. Tabletop gaming is a huge element of this full-spectrum geek event, and if you can catch the Acquisitions Inc. panel, you'll be able to experience what happens when tabletop RPGing becomes a fun spectator sport.

TAKE TIME TO PLAN YOUR CONVENTION

Depending on how large a convention you're attending, planning might be a straightforward thing, or it may feel like being a hungry man in a grocery store with unlimited money and no care for calories.

Before you look at the convention, think about how long you'll be attending and what you want to prioritize. Do you want to shop? Do you want to game? What is it that is motivating you to attend?

Vague statements like "I just want to experience it" won't do. Have specific intentions for the convention—it'll give you the ability to focus. For example, if your goal is to simply attend the convention to play a specific game, plan for that. Look at the schedule for the game you want to play, prepare the components you need to participate, and be deliberate and committed in your participation.

If, on the other hand, you're looking to try new games and experience many demos, plan for that. Games that are highly anticipated may have longer lineups for demos, so showing up earlier for those might help you skip lines.

If you want to shop in the vendors' area, budget for it. Prepare a list of the things you'll be looking to buy and settle on how much you're willing to spend. Sometimes you might have to prioritize that shopping list. It's easy to get caught on the convention floor, loaded with purchases you hadn't planned for, and miss out on the stuff you wanted. If you want a special and highly sought-after, con-exclusive product, expect it to sell quickly—meaning you'll want to be in line for it.

If you want to do all these things, create a timetable for it. Prioritize and build a schedule for yourself so you don't feel rushed. Sometimes you can't do everything within the limited time you have, so make sure you look at your priorities and are happy with them. Allocate time to travel from one event or convention area to another, which can take quite a long time in large conventions with big crowds.

The key to planning your convention is thoughtfulness and being clear about your intentions. That way you'll have clear expectations for your experience and you'll be able to get what you want out of the convention you're attending.

BE CLEAR ABOUT HOW TO SHOP FOR FRIENDS AT CONS

In a world where con-exclusive expansions and components exist, sometimes you will be put into an uncomfortable position of shopping for friends. Before you embark on being a game-stuff runner for your pals back home, you need some basic rules in place to make sure that shopping for friends won't hamper your experience.

Know Who Your Friends Are

If you're going to a big convention where there's stuff that is highly sought-after, you may find you suddenly have friends you didn't know you had. Some of them you may know in passing; others are mere acquaintances. Just remember: Not all friends are created equal.

The people you are probably willing to shop for are those whose relationship is meaningful enough to you that you'd go out of your way to do them a favor. I like using the moving metric: If I'm willing to help lift heavy furniture when this person is changing apartments, muling a few toys back for her in exchange for pizza and beer seems like a reasonable thing.

If it's someone you friended on Facebook because you see him occasionally at your FLGS, it might be less worthwhile. Why? Because you're giving up a part of your convention experience for him. Which brings us to the next rule.

IF YOU SHOULD FAIL IN YOUR QUEST . . .

Sometimes despite your best efforts you can't get the stuff on your friends' shopping list. In which case, e-mail or phone them from the con and give them back their funds (if you took them in advance) as soon as possible, in the same form they provided it to you.

Make Sure You Have the Time and Luggage Space

Let me be clear: *If you plan on doing this for your friends, make sure you budget time for it in the planning of your con experience.* There is nothing that can create tensions in friendships faster than feeling obligated to miss out on stuff you wanted to do because you committed to friends that you'd shop for (and stand in line to buy) toys for them.

Similarly, hauling stuff can cost money, particularly if what you're bringing back is bulky or otherwise sizable. This is especially true if you're travelling by air, since luggage space is even further limited and at a premium.

Decide How You'll Get the Item and How They'll Pay You for It

It's very strange that you lined up early, rushed around a convention, and hauled back stuff, and now it's been sitting in your house for weeks. Make sure you've got a decent idea of how you'll be giving your friends their stuff before you agree to bring it back for them.

If your friend lives far away, consider mailing the items to her from the city where the convention is being held. It will save you the stress of hauling it back.

You shouldn't be out of pocket for something like this, unless it's a gift (in which case none of these rules apply). If you see your friend regularly, you're quite likely to get paid back, but for other situations, it's usually better to get money in advance.

PREPARE A CONVENTION
SURVIVAL PACK

Attending a gaming convention, particularly a big one like Gen Con or Essen Spiel, is like making a holy pilgrimage. You're surrounded by gaming devotees expressing their love and passion; being in that kind of environment creates kinship and community. It can be a profound experience.

It can also be physically demanding in ways you wouldn't consider. Following are a few things you should pack to address your basic needs and ensure that your convention experience is ultimately a positive one. Most of this stuff can be carried in a pocket or a backpack.

1. *A pair of comfortable shoes.* You'll be surprised how much walking you'll do, from wandering the convention floor to finding your gaming event to shopping the vendors' hall. You'll also likely be waiting in lines: lots and lots of lines, particularly if you want convention-exclusive gaming accessories or gaming merch. As well, keep in mind that the floor of the convention hall is probably concrete, overlaid with a thin layer of carpeting. So be sure your shoes have soles that will help you withstand that.

2. *A bottle of water, snacks, and sandwiches.* Bring a refillable bottle and refill as you go. It's best to avoid sugary or caffeinated material like soda and energy drinks. The caffeine and sugar will irritate your bladder and interrupt

your gaming sessions with required potty breaks (or just leave you very uncomfortable for prolonged periods).

Snacks and sandwiches are always good to have on hand. Bring healthy options like fruit and nuts (apples and trail mix pack well). Carrying some sandwiches as a small, healthy meal option will keep you from bankrupting yourself by eating convention-priced food. It will also save you from the inevitable gastrointestinal problems later on in the day.

1. *A fresh set of underwear.* This may sound like advice from an overbearing mom, but give it a chance. When you're feeling tired, worn, stressed, and sweaty, changing your underwear can make you feel refreshed in a way that nothing else can. Pack the underwear in a ziptop bag so you have somewhere to stash the old set without contaminating the rest of your backpack's contents.

2. *A big fabric bag.* Some conventions may offer one of these, but I prefer using one bought from a grocery store. They are able to endure a pile of abuse and are immediately identifiable in a crowd (unlike a convention bag everyone else has). It's perfect for stashing any purchases made at the convention, particularly when you purchase games or expansions.

3. *A memory foam bathmat.* Convention chairs and concrete floors are the enemy of comfort, and if you're going to be gaming for hours, a cushy bathmat can save your butt. Whether you're playing games where you'll be sitting for the session or ones that require standing (like many

tabletop miniature or war games, where seeing the entire board is important), you'll appreciate having something under your butt or underfoot. Just fold it up and stow it in your backpack and you're ready to go.

4. *A cell phone charging cord and powerpack.* There's nothing worse than having to sit in a convention venue hallway next to a power outlet to charge your phone while gaming is happening around you. A powerpack will save you that inconvenience, allowing you to use your phone to connect with the gamers you meet, take notes on games you want to buy, or just capture a memory with a photo.

5. *A few pens and a small stash of index cards.* Whether you're passing secret information during a role-playing game to another player, or you're just giving contact information to someone whose cell phone is dead (that unprepared lout), a pen and index cards are universally useful. Don't forget to bring several pens—someone will inevitably ask to borrow yours and fail to return it. It's the lifecycle of pens at gaming conventions.

FOLLOW THE RULES OF CONVENTION ATTENDANCE AND GAMING

The basics of gaming previously covered apply to gaming at conventions as well. But there are a few other basics to help make the most of the convention experience so you can meet people, build friendships, and enjoy the gaming. Here are the conventions of conventions so your games and experiences go smoothly.

Be Cool about Names

When you sit around a table for a game with people you don't know, take the time to introduce yourself and learn the names of the people you'll be gaming with. Make a mental note to refer to people by their names. Heck, if you're bad with names, use one of your index cards to write them down so you can remember them. It's a basic social nicety that is often forgotten, but having that level of familiarity helps create a gaming atmosphere of both respect and fellowship. And people appreciate the effort. There's something truly warm when someone you just met makes the effort to learn and use your name.

On that note, making it easier for people to remember your name is an excellent idea. Many larger conventions give you a badge with your name on it, so wearing it in a way so that others can see your name is a fantastic idea.

Choose Appropriate Events

Your familiarity with the game (and its rules) is intrinsic to determining what kinds of events you play in. A gaming event that advertises itself as "fun and casual" will have vastly different expectations for your rules knowledge and approach to the game than one that describes itself as "competitive."

If you're playing in any sort of tournament, have a solid grasp of the rules and their nuances. You can expect your tablemates to be unforgiving concerning the interpretation of those rules, and they'll expect you to take actions decisively and expediently. "Competitive" means the fun is in the challenge, so your fellow players will expect you to be a challenge to your opponents and for you to be challenged by them.

If you're playing in pickup games, which are unranked but are a great way to get more of your favorite games in, you should be familiar with the structure of the game, its basic mechanics, and its victory conditions. Needing primers or clarifications and being forgiving of unfamiliarity with nuances in the game's rules is expected, so a casual and fun-focused approach is the right one.

If you're playing in demos or learning events, you don't need much—sometimes any—knowledge of the game, and the focus is on learning. All the players will probably make mistakes, and there'll be some forgiveness for less decisive actions and an incomplete understanding of the game's fundamentals.

Be on Time for Events

You learned about the importance of punctuality in Chapter 3: Essential Gamer Social Skills in the Be a Gracious Guest section, but being on time is even more important at gaming events. Of course, there is the possibility of distractions in the form of the vendors' hall, demo games, and meeting and connecting with new people. But you need to withstand all temptation to dawdle.

By being late and possibly preventing an event from starting at its scheduled start time, you not only impact the players of that game but possibly gamers for the rest of the day. If you're the reason a schedule at an event gets delayed, don't be surprised if people are unenthusiastic about playing with you.

Ultimately you want to be the kind of person people seek out to play games with in the future. Thoughtfulness toward the strangers you will be playing with gives you the potential to turn those people into friends in the future. You may just find yourself gaming after-hours or excitedly playing games with these people again in a later convention because you put the effort in to be a good convention gamer.

BEWARE OF CON CRUD

Con crud is the expression for the illness that most people inevitably end up getting after attending a convention. It sucks.

Avoiding con crud serves two purposes. First, it keeps you from feeling like a complete butt, which is always a good thing, and second, it keeps those you love and regularly spend time with from also getting an unwanted sickness. After all, they didn't even have the fun of attending the convention where you picked up the disease. You want to bring back toys, not bugs. Believe me when I say that your RPG group won't appreciate that kind of souvenir.

The basics of avoiding con crud are ultimately self-care and thoughtful hygiene practices.

Here are the ways you can shield yourself from this enemy:

Get Enough Rest

Lack of sleep wears down your body, which in turn wears down your natural resistances to sickness. As exciting as it is to pull gaming all-nighters, let's be real: You're asking your body to hate you. And more often than not, it will do just that.

Be Mindful of Food and Hydration

Hydrating serves several purposes. Water is essential to a lot of your immune system functions, particularly the mucous membranes in your mouth and nose. These catch and filter out illness-causing infiltrators of your body. Dehydration is bad, since drying yourself out keeps these natural barriers from protecting you.

Similarly, good-quality food is typically fresh. That means it's not preserved with salt and other additives that dehydrate and undermine your immune system. Fruits, nuts, and vegetables are great snacks to keep you both hydrated and energized throughout the day.

Clean Your Hands Often

Remember that hand sanitizer you packed in your survival kit? Use it often. Wash your hands often, and don't touch your face or ingest anything before you have. You're in a new environment with a host of new bugs your body may never have been exposed to before. Washing your hands and sterilizing them is key to keep from getting sick.

Being sick sucks, so taking care of yourself during the convention when you're feeling great is far better than trying to care for yourself after the fact when you're feeling terrible.

VOLUNTEER AT CONVENTIONS

Conventions run on the strength of countless volunteers who do virtually everything, from event setup and security to working at booths to running demos and gaming events.

Volunteering is an excellent way to get free admission to a convention, help a business or publisher you want to support, and meet new people. It's also a great way for you to serve the gaming community as well as benefit yourself. But in order to do that, you have to be excellent at it. So here are the rules for volunteering at gaming conventions.

1. *Own your role.* It's not enough just to show up. You need to kill whatever job you're doing with your best effort and attitude. Whomever you're working with and for will remember that and may invite you back in the future.

2. *Treat your volunteer shifts like you would a proper job.* Just because you're not getting paid doesn't mean you're free to act like an entitled goober. This means being respectful of the people who are giving you direction, being on time, and recognizing you are representing a company, organization, or event, not just yourself.

3. *Play to your strengths.* Pick volunteer roles that you know you're capable of doing and not hating. If you consider yourself shy, don't fill in the volunteer application saying you're willing to run demo games. Event setup might be more to your liking. You want to be helpful—that means

being upfront about your own strengths and how they can contribute.

Volunteering at conventions is an excellent way to get into the gaming community, build connections and relationships within it, and get into a convention without forking out a ton of money (which means more money for toys!). It also means being responsible. Remember: It is a volunteer role. You don't *have* to do it, but if you choose to do it, be excellent.

COMPETITIVE PLAY: THE DOS AND DON'TS OF WINNING FOR FUN

Competitive gaming—that is, played in an organized tournament structure—is a natural extension of the hobby. After all, many of us gamers feel the urge for competition beyond just a single game. Attending events that facilitate play beyond a single pickup game and reward players for consistently outstanding play is a fantastic way to soak up the feeling of achievement.

That said, there's a lot about competition play that is significantly different than casual play, and for that reason, etiquette at the gaming table becomes even more important. Competition play tends to generate higher expectations with regards to game mastery. The social contract for competition play is also different. Casual play tends to facilitate fun, sometimes (or usually) at the expense of strict adherence to the rules or a more competitive approach to the game. Competition play, on the other hand, means you're out to win. You understand that winning and trying to win is the path to fun. Playing challenging opponents who make you sweat . . . well, that's part of that fun.

So here are the basics for making sure you make the most of your competitive play experience:

Don't Let Any Single Game Paint Your Experience at the Event

Depending on how the event is set up, the player makeup of the first round may be randomly drawn rather than based on skill. That may mean your first game or two may not be as fun since you haven't yet settled into your bracket, where the most challenging and enjoyable games happen. Unless there's some sort of ranking system that's used prior to the event, you may end up at a table where you're either outclassed or outclassing your opponents.

In those cases you want to remember to remain engaged with the game and the event. I've heard horror stories of people rage-quitting events after their first games because things didn't go their way. They felt as though a single loss had put them out of the running for top awards. This is not only terribly childish, but it sets up a nightmare for organizers of the event, who scheduled based on a specific number of players.

Don't be a rage-quitter; focus on being engaged in the event. You may end up learning new things, growing as a player, or over-coming a loss to take a top spot.

Read the Rules As Written (All of Them)

Organized play relies on a clear set of rules that all players adhere to. That includes all ancillary information about the game and the structure of the event. That may also include rules that are available online in the form of clarifications, errata, FAQs, and bans of certain cards or pieces. Before you go into any competi-tive event, it is of utmost importance you gather all the available information and rules, read them, and understand them. You will be expected to know them and adhere to them. Moreover, you should keep a copy of all pertinent rules (including those ancil-lary ones just mentioned) on hand should you need to reference them or show them to your opponent(s).

Since everyone is expected to strictly follow the rules as written, sometimes interpretations of those rules conflict; some players may develop very slanted interpretations. In those cases, the disagreements will be resolved by an event organizer or judge rather than the players.

I once encountered a player who would cheat over distances in a game that involved precise measurement. He'd continuously question the distances of his opponent. The organizers eventually got so fed up with him constantly calling for rulings on measurement that they started uniformly ruling in the favor of his opponents. He established a reputation as a douchebag not only to other players but to event organizers in the region. Eventually he became unwelcome at the events in the region. Don't be that guy.

Know that the ruling of the judge when interpreting the rules or settling a dispute is final. Be as prudent as you can with your requests for a ruling. If you find that you're constantly calling over an organizer or judge, someone at your table has a problematic interpretation of the rules. It's also quite disruptive to constantly be calling for a rule settlement—organizers and judges usually have other duties to make sure the event runs smoothly. Be considerate of them as well.

It's Okay to Want to Win

Do your best. Bring your best game. But also bring your best self. Just because you're playing competitively doesn't mean you can treat your opponents poorly. Be fair and play within the rules, and keep the etiquette of how games should be played (like rolling dice fairly and announcing your actions) in mind. But try to win, and try to challenge your opponent. Competitive environments give you permission to game at a higher level.

That also means that your opponents have that same permission, so don't begrudge them for wanting to win. either. Further, don't judge your opponent's character based on her desire to win. Competitive players are often very genial and friendly people, but at a table where competition is expected, they may close up to focus on the game. Sometimes they come off as standoffish, cutthroat, or otherwise negative. Don't let that color your view of them.

Moreover, don't trash-talk players who are playing within the rules to win—winning's the point; that's what competitive and pinnacle gaming is about. It's very much like criticizing rain for being wet. It's both futile and petty.

Remember All the Etiquette from Earlier in This Book

If the rules of the game you're playing contradict social etiquette, follow the game's rules, but in all other situations, normal etiquette rules still apply to competitive play. Be a good winner, be a gracious loser, be decisive with your actions, be clear about your actions, and be transparent with your dice rolls, special in-game effects, and other things that you should announce. Clarity in gameplay allays perceptions of being a cheater. Competitive play does not give you permission to be the kinds of dicks you learned about in Chapter 3 (see the section on How to Deal with Different Kinds of Dicks).

Yes, sometimes someone will not follow the rules and guidelines detailed in this book. Suggest (politely) he buy a copy or twelve for himself and comfort yourself with the knowledge (and smugness) of being a better gamer and probably a better person.

Manage Your Expectations

In most games there can only be one top winner. There's only one Miss Universe and a bunch of runners-up sorted by numerical order. Not everyone can be the pageant queen, and not everyone can win the day.

And chances are that won't be you. That doesn't mean you can't have fun, learn as a player, grow as a strategist, and have personal goals within the event itself. Learn to feel accomplished without associating it with the top prize and find gratification in playing and participating. Set smaller goals. That might mean having a certain win record you're striving toward. It might mean aiming for a specific placing. Sometimes your goal is just not coming in dead last.

If you frame your own expectations for the event in a way that lets you have something to strive for while at the same time giving you a fair opportunity at it, you can walk away from any competitive event with your head held high. It will live in your memory as a positive experience. After all, games are supposed to be fun. It'd be a shame to see a day of fun turned to ash because you didn't win the crown and the sash.

At the end of the day, competitive play gives you an outlet to strive to be the best you can be; at the same time it gives you an opportunity to measure yourself against others who are good at the things you're good at. Those experiences can be very formative. They're a great way to meet new people to regularly play with and an opportunity to grow as a gamer. So make the most of it and do your best to make it enjoyable for yourself while being fair to everyone else.

PLAY IT PAINTED—RULES FOR GAMING WITH MINIATURES

Miniature war games are growing in popularity due to the explosion in the variety of games with high-quality components, popular licenses (like Star Wars), and the accessibility of model-making technology (such as 3D printing) to publishers of all sizes.

But gaming with miniatures is a different beast than other types of gaming. There are additional conventions that you should adhere to. So here are the rules to mini war gaming at gaming nights, events, and tournaments.

Play It Painted

Many miniature games come in unassembled kits that are unpainted. Part of this hobby is building and painting your miniatures. While games and events may not specifically require painted miniatures, it helps to put in the effort. Not only does it aid the immersiveness of the game (giving you the ability to imagine two unique forces squaring off), but it is a great practical way to personalize your army in a way you can be proud of.

Don't be dissuaded by the high-quality photos on the Internet or on the box—minis painted for such purposes are often painted to an incredibly high standard and their details are unrealistically painted to represent the model in photos that show the miniature many times larger than actual size. Tabletop quality is simply one where you apply paint to a model in a way that shows effort and pride.

The Clock Is Ticking, So Don't Waste It

Most miniature games are played within a specific time allotment. Sometimes it's a practical reason (a gaming store can only fit so many people in to game on their tables and thus limits the time it can have people at each table, or a gaming event has rounds and each round is allotted a certain amount of time).

Not only should you be mindful of the time you're taking to play a game and be decisive about your actions (you've already learned why slow playing is a no-no), but it also means that you should be similarly mindful of the time it takes you to deploy your force and also put them away so that the next players can quickly get to playing their game.

Get a Display Board or Tray to Easily Move Your Models

Not only is a display board a great investment to show off the minis you're proud of, it's also a practical and useful addition to any game that requires more than a handful of models. It also makes it easy to transport them from table to table.

Embrace Your Inner Pickup Artist

In the grimdark present of miniature war games, there is no stranger danger.

Pickup gaming is a staple of many miniature war games (and other games, too). Because they're often structured to be single-instance, two-player games, they're built upon the idea of meeting new players. This is part of the culture and community of many war games, particularly those that are most popular.

It may be out of your comfort zone, but don't be afraid of strangers. The game gives you a common element around which to bond, and provided you keep your gaming etiquette rules in mind as you play, you should find playing with strangers easy and enjoyable. And after your game, they are strangers no longer.

DITCH THE CLIQUE

Part of convention gaming is meeting new people; it's something you can't do as often in your FLGS. And you'll never be able to do it playing around your dining room table.

Whether you attend a convention with a group of friends, meet up with some friendly familiar faces, or hit it off with some people in the con, you may feel as though you should travel in a pack as you experience the convention. There's safety in numbers, after all. But that's actually very counterintuitive.

I met a group of gamers who were virtually married to each other during a con. They drove down together, they roomed together, they ate together, they took painting classes together, and of course, they gamed together. They played games they were familiar with, as well as tried new games. They may as well have been a chimera (a three-headed beast that moves as a single body) at every table they sat at to game. It made sense to them; they were close gaming friends who played regularly in a gaming den they built together in one of the guys' basements.

There were three of them, and many games are optimized for four players. So they dominated every table they sat at, which skewed the gaming experience of the person who occupied the leftover seat. And because they played together often, they knew each other well enough to play against each other's styles of play. For games they all regularly played, they might as well have been playing in their own basement. For games they were trying for the first time, they denied themselves the opportunity to assess the games individually, but instead developed a collective opinion.

This is all bad news for them. The one with the strongest personality tended to hammer his opinion into the others rather than letting them decide for themselves if a game was one they liked. Furthermore, they significantly reduced their chances to mingle and meet other gamers, which is a fabulous byproduct of attending gaming conventions.

Finally, this group of gamers dominated each game they tried together—so much so that it skewed the perception of the game for the other players. Atop the game these three guys were playing, they were also playing a metagame against each other. Being the outside player in this situation often means that players who are within a clique gaming with outsiders will be less thoughtful of those outsiders and will care less about their experience at the table. Adhering to your clique for all your convention gaming experiences could negatively impact someone else's convention experience. Don't do that.

Cliques are bad things to begin with, but gaming as part of a clique not only hurts your own gaming experience but also damages the ability for other attendees to make the most of their con.

Instead of gaming in a herd, you're better off going on your own, mingling with other gamers, and inviting people whom you don't normally game with to join your table. That's not to say you can't play games with friends when you're attending the same convention, but playing by yourself does give you a better perspective on any given game. It also gives you a chance to talk excitedly about games with your friends on the drive back.

So ditch the clique and instead try going out there and breaking away from the pack. Working as a lone ranger gives you a perspective on games that would work for you and your friends. As well, it lets you have the opportunity to care about the experience of players you aren't familiar with rather than favoring the enjoyment of your friends (which is understandable, but also avoidable).

And who knows? You may learn a new strategy for beating your friends at your most beloved games.

THE CONVENTION RULES ABOUT TAKING PHOTOS

With the supercomputers in our pockets containing built-in cameras, along with the proliferation of other kinds of digital cameras, taking pictures detailing all the amazing things you're seeing seems second nature. But before you hit the shutter button, think of the following rules.

If You're Going to Take a Picture of a Person, Ask Permission

Some people don't want strangers to take their photos. Some people have taken photos of other people that weren't in the least flattering to the person, the game, or its community. (If you're wondering what that looks like, Google "Magic The Gathering cracks.")

When asking a person if you can take his picture playing a game, be clear to him what your intention is for that photo. If you're doing it to showcase gaming at the con and/or the interest of people in a favorite game, most people will be okay with it. If you're taking a photo with or of a personal idol, they're sometimes fine with that. (Hint: taking photos of Wil Wheaton wandering a convention without his permission is not a good idea; asking him for a photo with you at his booth is.)

If You're Taking Photos of Crafted Components or Painted Miniatures, Ask Permission

Again, be upfront about why you want a photo. ("I'd love a photo of your Warhammer 40K army because I had a friend tell me your color scheme would never work, but you're proving him clearly wrong.") Just remember the rules of handling game components and getting touchy-feely with other people's games.

If You're Not Comfortable Articulating the Reason, Don't Take the Photo

Chances are, if you're embarrassed by why you're taking a photo, there's probably a reason for it. You might be planning to embarrass or mock, which is something we all know from grade school is plain mean.

Similarly, if you have no specific intended use, you're probably better off not taking the photo. If you want to post it online, be upfront about it, and most people will be okay with it. Otherwise, put the camera away and just enjoy the gaming at the con.

Respect the Right to Decline

If someone declines to give you permission to take a photo, that's okay. You'll move along with your life. She has every right to not accede to your request, and that doesn't mean you can take the photo in secret without her awareness. That's a total dick move, so don't think you can pull it.

Ultimately, what happens to the photos (and the depiction of the person/models) is out of the control of the person and in control of the photographer. That can make people uncomfortable for a variety of reasons, so you want to be thoughtful and respectful about it. Otherwise, you might have your camera confiscated because you couldn't respect someone's right to politely decline a photo of himself or his stuff. He may have one or many reasons for declining, but it doesn't matter: Don't be a creep-shotter when it comes to photo taking.

Read the Photography Rules of the Event

Some events are fine with general photos, but some may have a specific policy about it, especially events where game previews are done incognito.

One event I attended had a very high-profile licensed game to play, but nobody could take photos of it because the art hadn't yet been approved by the licensor. Even having the game out—which they were doing special for the fan attendees—would have gotten the publisher in deep trouble.

The last thing you want to do is have to deal with lawyers (they make things less fun when they're working), so be mindful of the photo policy.

In the end, use basic common sense when it comes to photos. It's not that different than the rules and etiquette you should follow when you game. Be thoughtful, be upfront, and follow the rules.

BE A GOOD GAME DEMOEE

Demo games are an opportunity for publishers to let people get a taste of a game—it's like a small bite of a big dish. It helps give people an overall impression of a game while not bogging them down with all the intricacies and nuances of the rules, which would be explained out of context.

When you approach a demo table, take the time to assess the game. Talk to the demoer about the kinds of games you like and don't like (using the vernacular of game mechanics and play styles). If she thinks the game will be a fit for you, she'll offer you a demo. If you tell her you don't like collectible card games and she's demoing a collectible card game, consider passing on the demo. Your time and the time of the demonstrator are both valuable.

When getting a demo game, don't expect to play the full rules for it, let alone the advanced ones. This is likely a scaled-down version to make it easy for demoees to experience the game in a short period. The point is for you to get a feel for the game so you can make a more informed decision. Think of it like food samples at Costco—you get a little but it's not a meal-sized amount.

Feel free to ask questions about the game, but hold them until the end of the demo if you're looking for general information rather than specific and pertinent mechanics. Let the demonstrator speak, and don't interrupt her, particularly if she's running a demo for a group of people outside your level of experience.

Obviously, if you're familiar with a game, don't do the demo. It's really bad form. It takes away time and effort the game demoer can be giving to someone who isn't familiar with the game. Moreover, if you see the demonstrator skipping rules, do not interject yourself into the game. She's giving a taste, not a full course.

I once was getting a demo of a miniature war game when a gamer who loves that game interjected because the demonstrator wasn't using the full rules; he interpreted that as playing the game wrong. He took over the demo and overwhelmed me with rules to the point that I was turned off of the game by the whole experience. While he loved the game, his insertion of himself into the demonstration killed the game for me. Don't be that guy.

Demos are a way for publishers to let people get a feel for their game. When you're at a convention, don't overeat at the buffet of demos. Instead, pick and choose the ones you think will be best for you.

10
TALKING ABOUT GAMES ONLINE

DON'T BE A TROLL

The Internet can be a pretty scary place. Opinions clash, arguments arise, and people end up comparing other people to Hitler. This tendency toward overgeneralization and rudeness applies to online communities, including communities where the topic of discussion is tabletop games.

At the same time, the Internet can also be a wonderful place where you can learn about various aspects of your hobbies, share your passions, and find kinship with people on the other side of the planet. That's pretty rad.

Recognizing this dichotomy is one of the most important preconditions for functioning productively on the Internet. Choosing to engage in a community filled with passionate and opinionated people requires a certain discipline and structure so you don't get sucked into situations where you are propagating your opinions without respecting anyone else's. It helps you avoid being sucked into situations of incivility. You want to share your knowledge, not argue with strangers.

This chapter is intended to help you be as awesome on the Internet as you are across a gaming table.

WRITE GAME REVIEWS THAT ARE USEFUL

Well-written and clearly articulated game reviews are a key element of sharing information about games with other gamers. As you grow your own library of games, you will develop opinions about games that can help people make decisions for their own collections. There are some ways to write a really great game review that's useful, whether it's full of praise or criticism. Follow these rules, and you'll come off as a brilliant gaming guru rather than an untrustworthy lout.

1. *Recognize there is no such thing as an objective review.* Your personal tastes will color your opinions; that's inevitable. That's why it's important to preface the review by being clear about the kinds of games you like. Knowing your tastes and stating them upfront will help better inform people who read your review. If someone recognizes your perspective as similar to her own, the review will be very useful to her. Giving a clear compass of your perspective will help orient any gamer who reads the review.

2. *Talk about both the positive and negative aspects of the game.* If you can't find any negatives, say so and give the game a glowing review. If you can't find any positives, the game is clearly not to your tastes. Spend the time explaining, using specific examples why this game doesn't suit you. There are some games that are much beloved and

very popular that I cannot stand, and there are games that I adore that just don't appeal to the vast majority of gamers. The key is to articulate the specific positive or negative aspects about the game.

3.   *Use the vocabulary of gaming.* After all, you're writing for people who are familiar with games. Employing gamer terms to describe the type of game and its mechanics (such as those listed within this book) will help other gamers have a frame of reference for how the game plays and what they can expect from it.

4.   *If your review gives a rating to the game, take the time to learn what the scale looks like.* Generally, top or perfect scores should only go to games that have a very wide appeal, would be an enjoyable experience for most gamers, have intuitive mechanics, and contain other elements that put the quality of the game over the top (including fantastic components, beautiful art, and a compelling theme). These are the kinds of games that will be classics and staples in collections. They may be the kinds of games you pass on to future gamers. Middle-of-the-road scores should be assigned to games that have a narrower appeal, have clunky mechanics that can be overcome by some other redeeming charm, and are games you would bring out for a specific group of players rather than a random mix. Low scores are reserved for games with significant flaws that hinder the game's enjoyment. They may be poorly designed, so unintuitive they're exceedingly challenging to learn and teach, or have some detrimental quality that is extremely hard to overlook.

WHAT A GREAT REVIEW LOOKS LIKE

Here's a sample review of a game called The Others:

Imagine a really fun dungeon crawl game, run by a game master, set in a universe that harkens back to the demon-filled lore of Diablo but is set in the modern day and you have a pretty good sense of The Others. Gamers familiar with the Zombicide series will find a lot of similarities in terms of mechanics (along with the same high-quality miniatures we expect of a Cool Mini game) but enough distinct elements to make The Others feel like a very different game. It plays with four people in about the same amount of time as Zombicide (about two hours, though admittedly less if your GM is particularly clever or bloodthirsty). If you like stunning minis, campaign-style mechanics, and the idea of fighting demons in the present day, you'll dig this game.

In the end, writing great game reviews not only helps you inform other gamers, but it helps refine your own tastes by crystallizing what you like and don't like in games. As such, it's a useful exercise for you as well.

BE HELPFUL, RATIONAL, AND SUPPORTIVE IN GROUPS AND FORUMS

When talking about games, it's important to recognize the kinds of conversations that are positive, useful, and helpful to people. This is opposed to the tar pits that quickly catch fire and burn everyone involved in them. The key to keeping things civil online and keeping you from falling into the tar pit is to act respectfully. You don't have to agree with someone else's opinion in order to treat it seriously. Here are the four kinds of conversations to which you can contribute positively, with minimal risk of catching on fire.

Give Advice When (and If) People Ask for It

If someone is soliciting gaming advice on a forum, feel free to jump into that conversation. Address the original poster first, rather than responding to the comments. If you choose to engage with other commentators, be respectful of their perspectives while making your own clear. Avoid broad generalizations ("All miniatures-based games suck!" "No one really likes old-style war games"), and never let the conversation descend into personal attacks when there are disagreements in opinion. Speaking of opinions, everyone, including the idiots online (who we won't call out but will mock in our heads), is entitled to his or her own.

Give Support

If someone is lamenting a loss she suffered or sharing a gaming situation that's less than stellar and you can sympathize, feel free to post support. Commiserating with other people online is a great way to build a rapport. Similarly, it's a great way to develop a reputation online as someone who is positive. When you help lift someone up, whether it's talking her up after she suffered a crushing defeat or providing some insight and personal experiences to give her some perspective that might help her in the future, you're performing a valuable service that the online community will appreciate.

Answer Rules Questions

When someone asks basic questions about a game, don't give him a standard RTFM (read the f*cking manual) response. Instead, cite the specific page of the rules that applies, and help him develop an understanding of the game. If it's a complex situation (such as when rules conflict), help guide him through how you'd sort it out. Never assume he's being lazy or an idiot. Sometimes the issue is the translation of the game's instructions, or a player may not be aware of a recent FAQ from the publisher, or maybe it's just a basic misunderstanding of the game's rules.

Discuss the Metagame

The metagame (or meta) describes how players play the game, what strategies are successful, and how prevalent these strategies are. While the Internet has facilitated the spread and dominance of specific metas throughout many competitive circles, some metas can be geographically limited: How a game is played (from a strategic standpoint) in one area is often different from how it is

> ## EXTINGUISHING THE FLAMES
>
> Sometimes to extricate yourself from an especially hostile conversation with a stranger online you need to walk away from the conversation. There's no reason to care about being right with someone whom you don't know. She or he is likely not worth your time and effort.

approached in another. The rules of the game remain the same, but the path to victory is often varied. Discussions of meta, where there is a recognition of the validity of all perspectives, is a great way to engage in conversation online. Most players recognize that most games can be won in a variety of ways.

Three Kinds of Gaming Forum Trolls

What a wonderful world the Internet would be if trolls only existed in nursery rhymes. Some people are never happy, and that fact is key to understanding and addressing trolls on the Internet.

For the past few years, one of my New Year's resolutions has been to argue less with people on the Internet. Some years I've been more successful than others, but something that has helped me not get sucked in is knowing the kind of trolls that hide under Internet bridges.

Here are three kinds of trolls you want to make sure you're not, as well as the easiest way to deal with them.

The Jilted Kickstarter Backer

I've seen more complaining about Kickstarter fulfillment in online forms in 2016 than any other topic online. It's millions of voices screaming at the same time, "*Where's my game?!?*"

Before we get into the details of this, let's be straight: Most Kickstarters don't fulfill by their estimated delivery date. Production issues, unforeseen costs, and other problems can delay the release of a game product by months—or longer. These risks that Kickstarter backers choose to take on are part of the Kickstarter experience.

Most Kickstarter backers understand and accept this. There may be some grumbling when a game is late, but for the most part its backers will be mild in their comments—especially if the Kickstarter project's initiators explain what's happening and when they expect the game to release.

For one variety of troll, though, there's no rational explanation that can please them. They'll start complaining about not having their stuff even when a company is transparent about the process and even when a company has a historical record of always fulfilling on past Kickstarters, despite hiccups along the way. Clearly, to the troll, what's going on is a conspiracy to cheat him out of his contribution to the project. Obviously, the project's managers are showing bad faith. It's completely obvious to anyone with half a brain.

Here's a hint: Complaining loudly about a Kickstarter project (or, for that matter, any other kind of crowd-funded project) on forums or Facebook pages will not help you get your game faster. It's about as productive as farting in the wind. If you really want specific delivery dates, e-mail the project initiator instead. The Internet is not a genie, and constantly wishing loudly won't have your wish or your backer rewards fulfilled.

If you really want to avoid being this jilted troll, consider buying the game from your FLGS when it becomes available.

The Fanboy

Being a passionate and enthusiastic evangelist for a game is a good thing, unless you start letting your enthusiasm put other people down or turn them off from the game you're advocating for. Fanboys are unable to rationally respond to (or even ignore) criticisms of the game, whether or not they're founded.

Sometimes critical dialogue between gaming communities and publishers is required—it's potentially important feedback, and if the criticism is fair, that conversation can help make the game better in the future. However, fanboys can't see that. Every criticism is an attack, not just on the game but on them. They start jumping down the throats of critics in order to ardently defend the game, its designer, or its publisher. Their worst feature is they make the community seem elitist, exclusive, and hostile. That's a bad way to be a champion for a game.

The Hater

This one is the counterpart of the Fanboy and just as obnoxious. One of the things that boggles my mind is when people join communities just to complain. The Hater can't recognize why others like a game. Like the Fanboy, he is unable to respect the opinions of others when they conflict with his own—except in this case his opinions are entirely negative.

Haters can't see outside the narrow confines of their own tastes. They join communities of people who are fans and immediately issue a litany of complaints about everything from the mechanics to the price. There's no pleasing a Hater; like every troll, he can't be reasoned with.

KNOW WHEN TO WALK AWAY

Sometimes, when a discussion turns heated, you and others partici-pating may be able to walk away while retaining respect for one an-other. After all, we're all passionate about games, and passion fuels emotion. But if the discussion turns personal, with name-calling and other forms of overheated negativity, that's the time to just step back and carefully walk away. That's a discussion that's going nowhere in a hurry.

If you ever encounter any of these types of trolls (or any new subspecies of online personalities that lessen the gaming com-munity), the way to address them is simple: Walk away. You can't satisfy them, and you risk letting them drag you into their cesspool by engaging with them.

Now if only I could learn to take my own advice, I wouldn't keep having to make the same resolution every January 1.

11 BEING A HOBBY CHAMPION

HELP OTHERS TO LOVE GAMING

If crafting or competitive play isn't your thing, you can always become a hobby champion, working to grow and spread the love of gaming.

When I got pregnant, it became impossible for me to actually participate in my hobby. Sitting in chairs for extended periods of time when someone was taking up residence in my body was far too uncomfortable.

So I did what any rational pregnant woman who missed her hobby would do: I started planning an eighty-person tabletop war-gaming tournament. Of course, because I had made this decision in a completely emotionally stable state, I went in completely prepared and wasn't at all out of my depth.

Not.

Just the fact that the project was ridiculous didn't prevent me from doing it. It took two years of planning to run my first event, and it was such a blast I did it again the year after.

It may seem as if the moral of the story is that you have to be as irrational as a pregnant woman to want to take on something big like hosting a tournament. That's not entirely untrue, but doing so is immensely rewarding. And it helps when you have someone around who's done it to give you pointers so you can skip the harder parts of embarking on any of these ventures.

WORK SUCCESSFULLY WITH PUBLISHERS

There are a lot of game publishers out there who have programs for volunteers who are willing to be community stewards for their games. Publishers may reward these volunteers with special expansions and models, and credits toward more games.

Most publishers advertise their hobby champions program (or however they brand them) on their websites, so if you have a particular love of a game, check out the site of its publisher. E-mail them to see if there's a program for you. If there is, they'll require you to prove your qualifications and go through a screening, but after that, you're in.

At the same time, volunteering for publishers has a set of expectations and standards that you must fulfill. Here are the ways to be a game's local champion.

Have a Good Relationship with Your FLGS

To be a great hobby champion, you'll need places that you can demo games, run events, and promote the game. While your basement may seem like a terrific gaming cave, inviting strangers over to try games there is exactly as off-putting as it sounds. You're trying to come across as a game champion, not a serial killer.

Make sure you have a great working relationship with local stores. Stop off at their events, support them, and be an advocate for them, so that when you ask them to host a demo night or gaming event, the staff will know who you are and be receptive.

Be a Good Representative

Whether you're demoing games or spreading the love of your games on Facebook, be aware that you're representing the publisher and the best of gaming. Expect to be held to a standard where you're inclusive, supportive, and always looking to convey a love of gaming. Don't be elitist or exclusionary; that kind of attitude only quashes someone else's interest or love for a game.

This includes what you post on social media networks, even outside your role as a game ambassador. Be aware of your audience and conduct online—it lives forever.

Make Sure You Have Enough Time

Usually in order to qualify as an official ambassador for a publisher, you'll have to organize and run a certain number of events or demo days. In addition to the time spent to run the event, you'll need to set up, organize, and plan it, which can take more time than you expected.

Publishers often give a lot of support and guidance to their hobby champions, but you've got to do the legwork, since you're the boots on the ground for their games. You may not need to know how to organize a competitive event, but with support from your FLGS and the publisher, you can quickly learn.

Being a hobby champion can be overwhelming if you have a lot of other commitments, but if you truly love a game and want to find more people to play it with you and enjoy it as much as you do, being a champion for it is the best way to do that. The benefits certainly outweigh the challenges.

LEARN TO BE AN ADVANCED DM

Chapter 8 covered the basics of dungeon mastering. As you grow into the role, you'll soon learn that there are many skills that make a DM great. Novice DMs can get through an adventure, but being a great DM or a professional DM (yes, it is a job—check out the sidebar) requires a skillset that goes above and beyond the basics. An exceptional DM is an actor, an improviser, a rules savant, and a great storyteller.

If you want to raise the game for your players, here are five rules you should follow.

Know the Story You Want to Tell

Great DMs know like the back of their hand the story, the setting, and the world that they're guiding their player group through. They know each NPC character beyond simply the words and script set before them and how said NPCs would react to the unexpected, and they are able to react when their players do things that are unanticipated. The ability to respond to players and the whackadoo things they try to pull is directly related to how much the DM knows the world and the story she's telling.

That often means fleshing out an adventure on the fly or knowing ways to bring players back to the path of the story without making them feel as though they had no choice.

Take Care of Your Voice

Great DMs do a lot of talking: describing scenes, narrating action, and characterizing and voicing various NPCs and foes. Too often, they strain their voices. If you're going to do voice acting when playing NPCs, make sure you have warm, soothing liquids for the night. You may also want to consider warming up your voice using various techniques specifically for vocal cords (you can easily Google them; singers and actors often employ them).

You have to be kind to your voice, particularly if your sessions are long and regular. It is not unheard of to have four- or five-hour weekly sessions. In those circumstances, the strain placed on your voice is extremely great. As I've advised you elsewhere in this book (though for different reasons), stay hydrated and take care of yourself. You are the key to a gaming session, after all.

GETTING PAID TO DM

Like many things in life, if you do something exceptionally well and there's a demand for it, there's often someone willing to pay you for your skills. DMing is no different. Some FLGSs will hire DMs (or pay staff members) to run RPG campaigns within the store as a service for their customers. Similarly, some freelance DMs will offer their services for hire to players who want to have a DM but have little experience within their group and are willing to pay for the shared experience. Some companies have business models structured around creating great RPG experiences: Roll20 is one such company; it has DMs on its staff who create campaigns for their users. Once again proving that if you're passionate and skilled at doing something, including gaming, you'll likely find someone willing to pay you for it.

Find Ways to Reward Player Immersion and Imagination

In the fifth edition of D&D, players can gain Inspiration tokens as a reward for playing the game in a way the DM appreciates (you can only have one Inspiration token at a time, and it gives you a bonus to a dice roll). It's a great way to reward players who are jumping into the spirit of the game, but it's not the only reason to reward players for contributing. Beyond rewarding players who continually demonstrate excellent role-playing, storytelling, and creative problem-solving skills, you also want to reward players who have made a clear effort and have shown improvement. As an advanced DM, you'll be able to recognize it as it happens, so you want to make sure you positively reinforce it.

Consider finding ways to increase a skill of a character or give him extra experience points when his player continually demonstrates skillful play. Similarly, you can find ways to explore a character's backstory, help her fulfill a personal quest, or make special equipment available to her.

Rewards such as these help players feel accomplished beyond the standard achievement of beating foes and gaining experience points. That's part of your job as a DM—to help players feel like they're actually accomplishing something and not stuck in one place.

Invest in Your DM Sessions

If you want to really make your games memorable, invest in ways to elevate the experience for your players. This may include crafting tablescapes for your adventures, but it can also include finding ways to create an atmosphere for your players.

Atmospheric music to set the scene is a great place to start, as is having visual references available for the various foes they'll face.

There are many auditory soundscapes you can download to help enrich your gaming experiences, from rowdy tavern background noises to creepy woods (complete with odd bumps and howls in the background) to drippy and echoey caves. Accessing what's available online will help make your campaigns all the more immersive for your players.

Similarly, you'll likely end up investing in a great number of references such as monster manuals, spell and equipment resources, maps, and other aids to help you in your DMing vocation. Beyond investing the monies (many resources are free, after all), you'll also want to put in the time it takes to become familiar with everything. And when it comes to creating monsters, items, or spells from your imagination, more investment in time (and potentially in an artist to create visual references for your creations) will also be in order.

Elevating your craft is a great undertaking, and the gratification it brings to you makes it a task worth undertaking.

Look at What Other DMs Are Doing and Borrow from Them

In this age of live streaming and broadcasting role-playing sessions online, you can find great DMs whose style and presentation you can incorporate into your own DM style. Matt Mercer of Critical Role, Wil Wheaton in his Titansgrave series, and Chris Perkins on Acquisitions Incorporated all have their own styles as DMs. Chris is a permissive and generous DM when the rules don't explicitly cover the actions his players want to do (like steering a flying dirigible into a dragon to impale it on the mast—he didn't know which skill was applicable for a skill check so he just gave it as a success). Matt is remarkably descriptive in critical rolls for killing blow (letting players choose the method of death and then narrating an epic finishing move for that action) and Wil's detail and focus on character development makes sense given his acting background (he worked with all his players in developing a rich backstory for all of them which informed all their actions and relationships in the game). Watch and listen to them, and feel free to borrow some of their techniques.

With Twitch and YouTube you can find some lesser-known DMs running adventures. Many of them have a style all their own that can inspire you to do things in a way that is more enriching to your players or easier for you as a DM.

There are so many resources available to DMs who want to share and learn from other practitioners to improve the play experience for their players. Online groups, websites, and blogs are all great ways to find and connect with other DMs and find new solutions.

In the end, being a great DM is like being great at anything: It takes dedication, time, and a willingness to go beyond what is prescribed. It also means learning from others and adapting your own approach to continually improve. It means going above and beyond, but it should also be something that is gratifying rather than something that feels straining. DMing is a vocation people do because they're called and compelled to from within, not because they feel outside pressure to do so.

ORGANIZE GREAT TOURNAMENTS AND EVENTS

If hosting a gaming night at your home is the homemaker equivalent to a dinner party, choosing to run a larger tournament or event is like choosing to plan your own wedding. Having done both, I promise you the analogy is very apt. With the benefit of experience (in gaming events, tournaments, and wedding planning), I can tell you that there are a few things an organizer should follow to keep from ending up in a puddle of stress-induced rage or tears on the nights leading up to the event.

Start with a Budget and Figure Out Your Costs

Everything needs a budget. You need to be realistic about your projections for the number of people who will be in attendance, and you should know the minimum number that will make your event work.

As well, you need to think about what costs you're going to incur. Costs you will want to think about include:

- Venue (if you have to rent a hall)
- Cost of required games as well as their components
- Rental tables and chairs
- Any licenses you need to obtain
- Prizes for the event

If you can find a decent workaround for many of these costs (like an FLGS that has the space, tables, and chairs or can provide prize support), all the better, but make your budget before you start doing anything else.

Determine How You're Going to Design the Event

For most competitive games or games with a culture built around events (for instance, Magic: The Gathering or Warhammer), you'll find that publishers have a tournament kit available. This makes running and designing an event straightforward and easy. Some publishers require you to work in partnership with an FLGS; that's fine, but if you can get your hands on an event kit, do so.

If you don't have a tournament kit, you may have to decide what things you want to reward players for. An annual event that is run to support a local food bank has awards for being top player (based on a points system that gives points based on game outcomes, with top players earning the most points) as well as the most sporting player, as voted by the other players. Bonus points are available to players who donate food, and these are scored based on quantities and the needs list of the food bank. Conceivably, players can compete by trying to see who donates the most food, since that's the point of the event. The notion is that the winner of any given event is the kind of winner whom the organizer is proud their system produced.

So if you want a system that rewards sportsmanlike conduct, design it that way. If you want a system where the most skilled player wins, design it so. Just be mindful of how the design is going to recognize players for achievement and what sort of achievement you want to reward.

Advertise Appropriately

In order for people to want to come to your event, they have to know about it. Spreading the news on social media, putting up posters (or even setting up registration for the event) at FLGSs, talking to podcasters/bloggers/vloggers/streamers, and asking registrants to tell people about it after they register are all really good ways to get the word out without costing too much money.

Ask for Help, and Thank Those Who Step Up to Do So

Here's the thing: If an event is bigger than a large dinner party (twenty people), you'll want help to run it. That means asking for volunteers. Things you'll probably want to ask for help with include managing the venue and game setup, registration of players, rules clarifications, and data entry.

In exchange for helping, you'll want to recognize your volunteers and thank them somehow. There are many ways to reward them—you could discount their registration costs, offer them special T-shirts, arrange extra entries for door prizes, or have a special draw of prizes only available to volunteers. You can even give them beer and pizza. It's not just about what you do; it's the fact that you took the time to be thoughtful of your volunteers in recognizing them that is the most important takeaway.

Give Yourself Time

When you are running an event, you will always be surprised how much there is to do in the two weeks before the event. Do as much organizing ahead of time as possible, so you don't have to do it the night before (thus avoiding the tearful, frustrated, sleep-deprived, stress-induced breakdown that often hits first-time event organizers). The more time you have to plan and organize, the less time you'll spend putting out fires, dealing with the unexpected, or trying to figure out a solution to a problem that should have never arisen.

If you're going to put yourself out there for the sake of the community, you want to make sure that you're doing things to preserve your sanity. Self-care is the key to running a successful event, so that means doing things like asking for help, spreading the word, and budgeting smartly (because doing the opposite might mean you're running an event purely out of pocket, which sucks and will likely burn you out).

BLOGGING, VLOGGING, AND PODCASTING ABOUT YOUR HOBBY

When you get to a point where your passion and involvement in your hobby is so great that you want to share it with the world, you should do so. There are so many outlets to creating content about the games and experiences of gaming nowadays and so many ways to connect with people as you do so that the only thing keeping you from doing so is you.

There are a few things you should know when you start broadcasting, though, to help get you connected with an audience who can respond and engage, but also so that you don't get yourself in legal problems.

So here are three easy-to-follow rules to help steer you in the right direction when it comes to content creation and broadcasting—toward an engaged audience and away from lawyers.

1. *Don't think of cost ever being a limiting factor.* The fact of the matter is that there are free ways to do everything when it comes to broadcasting online. If you're looking for free blogging sites, there are a plethora out there to choose from, the most popular being Blogger and WordPress. If podcasting is your deal, you can use a blogging platform to host your casts easily. Finally, you can create and share video content for free with sites and platforms like You-Tube, Twitch, and Periscope. If it's equipment you're lacking, be resourceful. You can take photos with your phone

for your blog, use your headphone mic plugged into your computer for podcasting, and use your phone or laptop webcam to make videos. You don't need top-quality stuff to make videos.

2. *Know your angle.* The best way to find your voice is to find a similar voice that isn't part of the hobby world that you can emulate on your platform. The podcast I help produce, *Jaded Gamercast*, is a miniature war-gaming podcast that emulates the style of the television show *Top Gear.* Similarly, my own YouTube videos are intended to look like those of makeup gurus, except I talk about games instead of makeup. Your voice is your own, but finding the structure and style that appeals to you but doesn't obviously copy someone else's style and approach is really important. Be unique, embrace your perspective, and find a way to convey it that is familiar yet different.

3. *Pay attention to fair use, copyright, and other legal minefields.* Nobody wants to get sued, receive a cease-and-desist order, or get hit with any other sort of legal complaint. The easiest rule to follow is this: Don't take content, photos, or images from the Internet that you don't have explicit written permission to use. Seems pretty easy, no? That goes for everything: music, photos, and video content. There are some exceptions to that rule: Creative Commons has created a license that allows people to use, remix, and share content without explicit permission. Based on what you're doing (mostly whether it's commercial or not), some people will allow their content to be used under a CC license. There's a plethora of music,

photos, and video content you can use provided you follow the licensor's requirements.

At the end of the day, creating content to share with the world is a big step. Whether it's a blog to share your hobby progress, videos demonstrating your proven strategies to winning your favorite game, or a podcast that reviews games available at your FLGS, letting your passion flourish while connecting with others who appreciate your point of view is validating. While growing your love of the hobby, you're also sowing the seeds of passion in others. That's a darned awesome thing.

CONCLUSION

It's easy to forget when we talk about games that we're actually talking about an experience that is premised on people. A game without a group is just a collection of wood pulp and plastic arranged in a particular way. It's useless unless a group of people use it with purpose. And that purpose is fun.

Optimizing for fun, making things fun for you and the people you game with, and making decisions to prioritize the experience around fun is the ultimate point of everything covered in this book.

Our hobbies are the way we invest in ourselves, our community, and our fun. So as you venture into—or deeper into—the realm of gaming, don't forget to be thoughtful, be kind, and focus on the fun.

ACKNOWLEDGMENTS

I have to start by recognizing my mother, Teresita, who not only birthed me but taught me how to write and read, and instilled a love of stories and storytelling in me. On a similar note, I have to acknowledge the men in my family: my father, Prudencio, who taught me how to play chess before I could ride a bicycle; and my brothers, Frank and Hector, who not only were willing to play games with me *ad nauseam* but stoked the fires that would become my love of games, competition, and everything geeky.

I also have to thank the wonderful people at Geek & Sundry, who have given me both support and a platform to share my passion and love of games. Similarly, I have to recognize all of my supporters, from YouTube subscribers, Facebook friends, and Tweeps out there who have sent their support, shared their passions, and given me the opportunity to speak to their hobbies.

To the fine folks at F+W Media: thank you for your hard work and willingness to roll the dice on a geeky writer.

Last but most importantly, this book would not be possible without the love and support of my husband, Nathan. He opened up the world of modern gaming to me by first introducing me to Warhammer 40,000 and continues to this day to indulge me in late-night gaming on our dining room table. Nathan: You are my partner in all things, and words fail to express my enduring gratitude and love for you and all you do.

INDEX

Action games, 19, 22–23
Adventure games, 22–23

Bluffing games, 17
Buying games, 25–30

Campaign games, 107, 118, 140–46, 211
Cards, drawing, 94
Cards, revealing, 99
Cheating, 66, 86, 90, 93, 101, 181
Children, 138–39
Cliques, 187–89
Collectible games, 14–17, 94, 120
Complex games, 56–59
Conventions
    attending, 162–94
    cliques at, 187–89
    demo games, 193–94
    gaming at, 162–63, 169–74, 179–86
    hygiene for, 175–76
    photos at, 190–92
    planning, 164–65
    rules of, 172–74, 190–92
    shopping at, 166–68
    survival pack for, 169–71
    tournaments at, 163, 173–74, 179–83
    types of, 162–63
    volunteering at, 177–78
Cooperation games, 17–18, 131, 143
Cost of games, 27, 30–31
Counters, 45–46
Creativity, 23, 65, 138, 159, 210

Demo games, 53, 174, 193–94, 206–7
Designer games, 13
Dice abbreviations, 46, 142, 144

Dice, rolling, 87–89
Dungeon master (DM), 14, 141, 157–61, 208–12

Elimination games, 19
Etiquette, 7–9, 21–24, 33, 109–12, 181–82. See also Social skills
Events, organizing, 116–27, 205–18

Family game nights, 130–39

Game components, touching, 80–81, 191
Game components, trading, 92–93
Game length, 26–27
Game master (GM), 14, 141
Game mechanics, 16–20, 44–49, 85–101
Game nights
    family game nights, 130–39
    food/drink for, 105, 125–27
    hosting, 116–29
    inviting guests, 116
    organizing, 116–27
    party games, 13–14, 118
    sharing games, 117
    space for, 123–24
    success of, 128–29
    theme nights, 117
Game publishers, 206–7
Game reviews, 192, 196–98, 218
Game types. See also Games
    action games, 19, 22–23
    adventure games, 22–23
    American-style wargames, 13
    bluffing games, 18
    campaign games, 107, 118, 140–46, 211

collectible games, 14–17, 94, 120
cooperation games, 17–18, 131, 143
designer games, 13
elimination games, 19
European-style games, 12–13
hybrid games, 13
luck games, 17
miniature games, 14–15, 184–86
party games, 13–14, 118
player judging game, 20, 23
role-playing games, 14, 140–61
storytelling games, 19
stress-inducing games, 23
wargames, 13
worker placement games, 19
Gamers
    engaging, 21–22
    hurt feelings of, 21–22
    issues with, 64–68
    nongamers and, 133–34
    social skills for, 60–84
Games. See also Game types
    borrowing, 81–83
    buying, 25–30
    complex games, 56–59
    cost of, 27, 30–31
    hosting, 33–34, 77–79, 116–29
    learning, 40–59
    lending, 81–83
    length of, 26–27
    mastery of, 56–59
    mechanics of, 16–20, 44–49, 85–101
    playing, 16–20
    protecting, 119–22
    rules for, 42–47, 150–61, 184–86

setting up, 26
storing, 28–29
taking down, 26
teaching, 40–59
time limits for, 57
trying, 25–30
Gaming aids, 44–47
Gaming forums, 195–204
Gaming groups. *See also*
  Hosting games
  clashing personalities in,
    113–14
  disagreements within,
    109–14
  drama within, 104–5,
    109–14
  dynamics within, 104–5
  finding, 107
  food/drink for, 105, 125–27
  game nights for, 116–29
  guidelines for, 102–15
  new experiences with, 104
  social skills for, 102–5
  starting, 106–8
Gaming space, 123–24
Gaming stores
  culture of, 8–11
  deals at, 35–37
  finding, 9–10
  focus of, 10–11
  gaming groups at, 106–8
  hosting games at, 33–34,
    77–79
  location of, 10–11
  relationship with, 206–7
  supporting, 7–8, 30, 35–37,
    206–7
Guests
  alcohol consumption and,
    75–76, 78–79, 126–27
  food/drink for, 105, 125–27
  furnishings for, 123–24
  inviting, 116
  social skills for, 77–78, 128,
    173–74

Hobby, sharing, 205–18
Hosting games
  food/drink, 105, 125–27
  for game nights, 116–29
  at gaming stores, 33–34,
    77–79
  inviting guests, 116
  party game night, 118
  sharing games, 117
  success with, 128–29
  theme nights, 117
Hybrid games, 13
Hygiene, 31, 73–76, 175–76

Learning techniques, 40–59
Losers/winners, 69–72, 113
Luck games, 17

Mastery techniques, 56–59
Mechanics of games, 16–20,
  44–49, 85–101
Miniature games, 14–15,
  184–86
Movement, announcing,
  100–101

Negotiation, 92–93
Nongamers, 133–34

Online communities, 195–204

Party games, 13–14, 118. *See
  also* Game nights
Player judging game, 20, 23
Points, scoring, 35, 45, 95–96
Promptness, 77–78, 173–74

Reference cards, 45–47
References, 44–51
Respect, 31–32, 38–39, 84,
  102–5
Revealing cards, 99
Role-playing games (RPGs)
  basics of, 140–41
  characters for, 142–56

description of, 14, 140–41
dice for, 144
dungeon master for, 14,
  141, 157–61, 208–12
game master for, 14, 141
playing techniques, 144–60
rules for, 150–61
universe for, 143
Rules, for conventions,
  172–74, 190–92
Rules, for games, 42–47,
  150–61, 184–86. *See also
  specific games*

Scoring points, 35, 45, 95–96
Social skills
  etiquette, 7–9, 21–24, 33,
    109–12, 181–82
  for gamers, 60–84
  for gaming groups, 102–5
  for guests, 77–78, 128,
    173–74
  respect, 31–32, 38–39, 84,
    102–5
Storage tips, 28–29
Storytelling games, 19
Stress-inducing games, 23

Teaching techniques, 40–59
Tokens, moving, 45–46,
  100–101
Tokens, touching, 80–81, 191
Tournaments, organizing,
  205, 213–18
Tournaments, playing in, 163,
  173–74, 179–83
Trolls, 195, 201–4
Turn sequences, 44–45,
  90–91, 97–98

Wargames, 13
Winners/losers, 69–72, 113
Worker placement games, 19

ABOUT THE AUTHOR

Teri Litorco is a tabletop- and war-gaming geek who is a contributor to Geek & Sundry. She also cofounded and cohosts *The Board Dames*, a female-hosted tabletop podcast, and broadcasts on her own YouTube channel.

She has a high tolerance for luck, being a miniature war gamer, but also loves modern hybrid tabletop games. At the time of this writing, she'd never decline a game of Blood Rage, Space Cadets, Malifaux, Warmachine, Wrath of Kings, Bushido, or Star Wars: X-Wing Miniatures Game.

She has never slapped a player she's played against, though she's often thought of slapping her husband, Nathan, when she does play him. They reside in Canada with their daughter, Elora.